W9-CFB-162

DOGTOLOGY®

Live. Bark. Believe.

GREENLEAF
BOOK GROUP PRESS

Published by Greenleaf Book Group Press
Austin, Texas
www.gbgpress.com

Distributed by Greenleaf Book Group

For ordering information or special discounts for bulk purchases, please contact Greenleaf Book Group at PO Box 91869, Austin, TX 78709, 512.891.6100.

Design and composition by Greenleaf Book Group
Cover design by Greenleaf Book Group
Illustrations ©Steve Feldman 2015
Cover photos ©iStockphoto/igorr1 & ©iStockphoto/jonhortondesign

Cataloging-in-Publication data is available.

ISBN 13: 978-1-62634-138-8

Part of the Tree Neutral® program, which offsets the number of trees consumed in the production and printing of this book by taking proactive steps, such as planting trees in direct propor-tion to the number of trees used: www.treeneutral.com

TreeNeutral®

Printed in the United States of America on acid-free paper

15 16 17 18 19 20   10 9 8 7 6 5 4 3 2 1

First Edition

DOGTOLOGY

Dog· tol· o· gy

noun

1 The belief in Dog.
2 The system of rituals, practices, and behaviors engaged
   in by Dogtologists.

LIVE. BARK. BELIEVE.

This book is for practicing Dogtologists the world over. Are you among the faithful?

- When watching a movie, you are more concerned about a dog being harmed than an entire city of humans being wiped off the map.

- You've bailed on a date because you didn't want Twinkles to be home all alone.

- Your dog owns a more festive holiday wardrobe than you do.

- Your smartphone contains more pictures of dogs wearing sunglasses than of your human family.

- Your pup dines on free-range bison burger; you're living off Top Ramen.

Welcome to the fold!

CONTENTS

IN THE BEGINNING . . .

God created the heavens and the earth.

And God said, *"Let there be light."*

And light there was.

God saw that the light was good, and He said, *"Let the land produce vegetation and let the water teem with life and let birds fly above the earth and—"*

Wait! (Sound of needle screeching across the record.) Sorry, wrong book.

Jumping ahead a creational week or two . . .

God did not necessarily plan for creation to be completed in one fell swoop. After all, if Earth wasn't going to produce any new surprises along the way, then what was the point of creating it in the first place? Might as well have just written a memo. Instead, God created a process for the world and its inhabitants to evolve and reveal their surprises over time, which allowed Him to continually wheel out exciting new creative ideas and tweak them on the fly.

For example, God particularly enjoyed messing with the four-legged beings. He'd already tried and retired many early models like the *Suchomimus*, for instance—which looked like a pair of vise grips stuck in an alligator's ass. But God had yet to start churning out the truly bizarre things like the duck-billed platypus, the naked mole rat, or the blob fish (look it up). God was, you might say, at the height of His creative powers.

One partly cloudy Wednesday afternoon, while tinkering in His Earth Species Progression and Advancement Lab (ESPAL), God brought into existence a creature that pleased Him as no creature ever before. This four-legged being was playful, intelligent, sweet, and oh so damn cute. One look in its eyes and you could see to the depths of its soul; look again and you would feel as if it could see into yours. The little creature had a nose that could smell a mouse burrowed in a hole a mile away, ears so sharp they could hear grass photosynthesizing, and a sense of empathy so keen it could detect if a tree was depressed. It could run like the wind, jump like a jackrabbit that accidentally sat on a cactus, and pivot like a deer U-turning from a charging grizzly.

It lived fully in the moment and romped happily in heaven's green gardens, chasing squirrels and staring out in wonder at the verdant vistas God had created. This bundle of fur had a caring, noble nature and was loyal to the core. It was humble, unselfish, encouraging, infinitely loving, and one of the best silent conversationalists God had ever created.

And so God said, *"At last, I have created a being that reflects all that is good in me. Thus, I shall give it a name that is the mirror image of my own."*

And so God named this new creature *"Dog."*

Dog liked his name and licked the face of God in gratitude.

"I will loose you on the earth," said God to Dog, *"and you shall be my avatar."* Dog cocked his head in adorable confusion. *"You know, my representative. You're me when I'm not there."* Then God winked and added, *"You and I are going to have some great fun, Dog."*

Dog wagged his tail excitedly, because Dog was seriously down with the idea of having fun.

Project Man

Dog was eager to explore his earthly existence. But there was one thing missing: Dog was a highly sociable critter and did not wish to romp the earth alone. Although he knew how busy God was tweaking and adjusting His ongoing creations, Dog longed for a companion to play with, to hang out with, and to edge off the sofa. Dog desired to be petted and cuddled and to spread joy and occasional mayhem when needed. Dog whimpered about this conundrum and pawed at the legs of God. God, however, was busy figuring out whether humans should have two arms or four and became so distracted by Dog's whimpering, he accidentally put nipples on the male version. Dog resorted to his ultimate weapon: He put on the sad face.

And it worked!

God said to Dog, "*I know what you need, young Doggie. A companion to play with and to scratch you in that particular place on your belly in a way that makes you look like you're trying to start a motorcycle.*"

Dog jumped up and down excitedly. "*Now you're talking!*"

God added, "*I have given this a great deal of thought. Earth is a garden of paradise. But, let's face it, it's also a bit of a gore fest, what with creatures gnawing on one another and fighting tooth and nail to control their own patch of real estate. Take your cousin, Wolf, for example. Wolfie has many of the same fine qualities you do, but he spends all of his time hunting and protecting his young. So, Wolfie's talents, such as howling at the moon at night (because he thinks his breath keeps it floating in the sky), have never had a chance to evolve like yours have. He's just too busy surviving. You, on the other hand, Doggie, are too special for such an existence. Therefore, the companion I will give to you will be as perfectly suited to you as you will be to him.*"

"*Bring it on!*" thought Dog. "*So, what are we gonna call this creation?*"

"*I'm going to call him Man,*" God said.

"*Man? Great name! Short and to the point. You're brilliant! I love it, love it, love it!*"

"*Man will take care of your survival needs, dear Dog,*" God continued, "*so you won't have to.*"

"*Yes, yes, yes!*" Dog panted, his tail whipping back and forth in a frenzy, joyously anticipating the arrival of Man. He was so happy he even peed a little on the cloud below.

"*Man will be a most intriguing creature,*" God added. "*He will have a nose and ears that are nowhere near as powerful as yours.*"

"*What! Why?*"

"*Because that way, he will need you to sniff things out for him and hear things he cannot hear and he will be impressed by the heightened ability of your smelling and hearing.*"

"*And give me treats? Oh, God, this is just off the hook! I love it!*"

"*He will have almost no fur at all. Just some small patches. In a few strategic places.*"

"*Patches? Strange.*"

"*Not sure what I was thinking there.*"

"*Wait, wait, I get it! That way I won't have to scratch him, and he can stay busy scratching me!*"

By now, Dog was nearly delirious with God's sheer brilliance.

God continued: "*Furthermore, Man will behave in ways that even I will find perplexing. But Man will be able to do many wondrous things for you. You see, he will have a very large brain, much bigger than it will need to be, because he will use so little of it. His brain will get him into all kinds of trouble, but it will also be a great boon to you.*"

Boon. What a cool word, thought Dog, *sounds like bone*—and Dog totally lost track of what God was saying.

"*For example, Man's brain will conquer the elements and invent machines to do his work for him. This will free him up to . . . um . . . er . . . invent even more machines to create even more work for him. But it will also free him up to play with you and take care of you and have fun with you.*"

Dog let out a yip of joy. This Man stuff was starting to sound promising.

"Man will also have incredible appendages called hands," God went on. "These 'super-paws' will allow him to perform tasks that are tricky for you to do. Tasks like opening gates, untangling ropes, rubbing your belly, throwing sticks and balls, and scratching you behind the ears."

Now Dog was grinning ear to ear.

"Man will stand on two feet and will thus be able to reach treats on high shelves. These feet of his will also be able to kick a ball like nobody's business. Man will build nifty shelters with heat, running water, and refrigerators that keep hamburger fresh for days. He will share these shelters with you. Man's clothing will have pockets, and in these pockets he will keep treats and money. This money will buy fun things, like more treats and beach admission. Man will also drive machines called cars, which you will find to be the most amazing things."

Dog tried to imagine a car but got stuck on the image of a carcass. Carcasses could be pretty tricky to drive. Dog knew—Dog had tried.

"Man will also find you irresistibly cute. And puppies? Don't even get me started on the junior versions of Dog! Man will also be a pretty dandy playmate and sofa snuggler."

"What about walking in the woods with me?" Dog queried.

"Yes, he'll do that, too. Though you will have to do all the sniffing. Oh, and all the peeing on trees and rocks. Man claims his territory with fences and walls, not with your more fluid form of demarcation."

"What about playing ball? That's major."

"Yes, Man will love to play ball as much as you do. In fact, Man will give you so much attention that, over time, you will learn to use him to do all sorts of things for you. He will lift you over fences, buy you juicy new bones, and cause fire hydrants to sprout along the streets. Man is going to be the most sophisticated gadget you could ever imagine. He will solve endless problems for you. You will run, play, herd, watch the world go by, celebrate the glory of Earth's gardens, and, most of all, give away your love. Freed from survival concerns, you can be the true athlete, hero, guardian, and spiritual master I created you to be."

"Sounds great!" Dog rumbled contentedly. "When do we start?"

"There's just one small . . . er . . . hitch," God said. "But isn't there always? This Man creature . . . There's another side to him. After all, even I cannot create a coin with only one side."

Dog flopped down on his side and let out a huff of annoyance. "What's the hitch?"

"Man will have a very large and very fragile ego. His ego will tell him that he is the most intelligent, most powerful, most important creature in all of existence. His ego will even tell him that the bed is his, not yours!"

"I thought you said he was smart?!" Dog howled with confusion.

"This ego of Man's is a necessary evil, however, because it will serve a practical purpose, too. It will keep Man busy and productive. You see, many of Man's coolest accomplishments will be motivated by a need to feed his ego. Without the ego, Man would stop working, inventing, saving, planning, driving, and building stuff, which would render him pretty useless to Dog."

Dog tried to understand this concept called ego, but couldn't wrap his furry head around it.

"There's more," explained God. "Man can write symphonies and poems that melt your heart, and can sing like only the angels can. He can unravel the mysteries of time and space. He can sometimes be incredibly generous and caring. Underneath all of his arrogance, he has a beautiful heart. In fact, if his ego didn't get in the way, making him so fearful and selfish and grandiose, I think he could be almost as good as you. . . . Well, not really, but close. So I'm asking you one favor."

"Name it, God."

"In order to partner with Man, you will have to play his game," said God. "You will have to let him believe he is the superior being. What I'm saying is this: You'll have to let him play boss."

Dog thought about this concept for a moment. What a challenge it would be to allow this (mostly) furless, ego-riddled, paddle-footed being with a terrible nose and ears to believe it was superior to Dog. But Dog *loved* a good game! And this game sounded fun. Besides, Dog had no ego, so he didn't mind taking one for the team.

If Man needed to believe he was boss, so be it, as long as Dog could sleep in a warm bed, eat treats, and chase the ball . . . What more was there to life, really?

"*As your faithful companion,*" God said, "*Man will do much for you. Not only will he care for you and play with you, but over time he will elevate you to a deified place in his world. Right up there with those humans Man will call 'movie stars.' He will adorn his home with images of you, he will place you at the center of his songs and stories, he will create bone-shaped water dishes and paw-shaped 'pupcakes' for you, he will build entire industries devoted to your care and amusement—at least, he'll* think *it's for your amusement, but it's really for his.*"

"*Hey, if there are still treats involved, then I'm your Dog.*"

"*But there's one other thing,*" said God.

Dog wasn't paying attention because he was now feverishly nipping at his own back leg.

"*I ask that you raise Man up. Help him become his best possible self. Allow your goodness to rub off on him. This won't require special effort from you. You see, when Man is with you, his highest qualities will naturally emerge. But there is* one *thing you will need to exercise in spades. Patience. Project Man is going to take a long,* long *time, Dog. . . . We're talking thousands of years.*"

That's okay, thought Dog. *Time's not an issue for me. Never was, never will be.* Dog raised his paw to God. *Deal.*

God shook Dog's paw and said, "*Excellent. Then let's get this thing rolling. Oh, one last thing. Let me give you a little tip. Actually, this is huge—you'll get more mileage out of it than you can imagine. Man will be* very *easily amused by you. All you'll need to do to keep him laughing for hours is to act like him in any way, shape, or form. Put on one of his hats, wear a sweatshirt or sunglasses. Dance on two legs, sit behind the wheel of his car, pretend to read one of his books, jump on things they'll call skateboards and let him make YouTube videos of it—you'll know what I'm talking about when the time comes. You'll have him laughing so hard he'll give you anything you want.*"

Dog panted and grinned excitedly up at God.

"*Okay,*" said God. "*This is the part where I say 'Let it be so.'*"

And then God kicked back on His lounger, grabbed some popcorn, and chuckled, "*This is gonna be awesome!*"

THE BOOK OF BONES

The "Bones" of Dogtology: Its Definition, Its Roots, and (Oh, Just Say It) Its Dog-ma

I. The Belief in Dog

Every human believes in *something*. Some believe in a "supreme being." Others believe in the supremacy of science. Some believe in creationism, others in evolution. Still others believe in nothing whatsoever. (These tend to be the most ardent believers of all.)

Many of humankind's deepest beliefs have evolved into systems of thought and national institutions. For example, hockey is the official religion of Canada. Some beliefs are held only temporarily, such as belief in Santa Claus or the Easter Bunny or jobs with pension plans. Other beliefs can last a lifetime, such as the belief that bacteria observe a five-second grace period before jumping onto a nacho chip dropped on the kitchen floor. Some belief systems—be they political, social, or spiritual—have popular names and are openly embraced by billions of human beings around the world.

Then there are beliefs that are practiced with unwavering devotion, even though their followers may be completely unaware they are practicing an official faith. Dogtology is one such faith. In fact, it's one of the most practiced beliefs on the planet and has been gathering momentum ever since the first canines came sniffing around the first human campsites looking for fresh bones and leftover livers.

Just as electricity existed long before Man named it "electricity," so too did Dogtology exist before being named.

And now, at last, Man's longstanding, fanatical devotion to Dog has an official name: Dogtology.

So what, exactly, is Dogtology?

Although dog-love is a base requirement of all card-carrying Dog-tologists, the system of belief is more than just the love of dogs and acknowledgment of the effect they have on us. Dogtology is a belief that recognizes Dog as a genuinely "elevated" being. Dogtologists aren't just fond of dogs; they *exalt* them ("worship" is too strong a word . . . but not by much!).

If you are a Dogtologist, here are just a few symptoms of your belief system:

* You relentlessly email dog photos, dog-toons, dog videos, and dog PowerPoint slideshows to everyone on your contacts list, regardless of the thundering silence you receive in response.

* Your dog groomer knows that the concept "drop the dog off" does not apply to you, and you are allowed to wait in the staff lounge where you are given status reports on the quarter hour.

* You are genuinely surprised when others react to the word "bitch" as if it has negative connotations.

* After seventeen years of marriage, you can't get the names of your in-laws straight, but you can remember the names of the last twelve Westminster "Best in Show" winners, along with their sires and dams. (Also, you know what sires and dams are.)

* You understand the sole purpose for which cell-phone cameras were invented: to capture cunning and hilarious shots of dogs behind the steering wheel of cars . . . wearing sunglasses . . . and Scottish beanies.

* You give holiday gifts to *and from* your dog—and you spend more time getting these exactly right than you do your gifts for humans.

* You send *only* greeting cards with pictures of dogs on them. (For

example, if there are 139 possible card choices at Walmart, you will choose the one that says "Muzzle Tov!" or "Happy Bark Mitzvah!" even if the event being acknowledged is a death in the family.)

* You happily purchase "gourmet" treats, such as "pupcakes," "Na-*paw*-leons*," or "tail mix bars" for your hound (at a retail markup of a mere 750 percent).

* You decorate your wallet, iPad cover, watchband, stationery, briefcase, laptop computer (both cover and wallpaper), mousepad, and car upholstery with little icons of paws (for Dog forbid the concept "Dog" should vanish from your consciousness for one nanosecond).

* After you issue a command to your dog, you offer the dog a detailed explanation as to your rationale, then follow it up with a Q&A session in an attempt to diminish any psychological damage the harsh order might have caused to the dog.

* Recipients of your annual Christmas form letters don't know if you're married or divorced or how many kids you have, but they do know the approximate length and girth of your dog's healthy poops and when your dog is due for its next rabies booster.

And that's just the tip of the iceberg. In short, if future archaeologists were to dig up your home and catalog its contents, they would conclude without hesitation that Dog was your central object of religious devotion. (And if you're honest with yourself, you would have to admit they wouldn't be far off the mark.)

The veritable shrines humans build to their dogs—in their homes, around their communities, and in the media—are proof positive that Dogtology is indeed a *bone*-a-fide belief system that stands proudly alongside all the other great *-isms* and *-ologies* of the world. Dogtology, as understood by practicing Dogtologists, can be defined as:

The unconditional, loving belief in Dog as a superior being and, in many ways, Man's savior.

Chew on that one for a while.

II. In Dog We Trust

In order to understand the true spirit of Dogtology, one must examine how humans practice other important beliefs in their lives. Humans *say* they believe in many things, but if they're completely honest with themselves, they have to admit that sometimes they can be pretty selective when it comes to putting their money where their beliefs are. Not so with Dogtology.

Many Dogtologists don't consider their way of life a formal belief system or religion, but they do actually apply their Dogtological beliefs in a systematic way, whether or not they're aware of it. And they do so with the type of unfettered joy one reserves for eating a hot-fudge sundae, shopping for that special dress, romancing the perfect woman, or imagining we're saving 50 percent on mayonnaise by buying the fifteen-gallon tub at Costco.

Day in and day out, all around the world, human beings organize their lives around dogs. Belief in Dog is one thing that never wavers in a Dogtologist's life. Nothing "appalling" that a dog ever does— e.g., chewing up a wallet right after you've stocked it with fresh cash; biting a litigious neighbor on the rear as he's bending over to look in his mailbox; decorating the yoga mat with runny doo; or barking all night at a shovel stuck in the ground—is enough to shake a Dogtologist's faith one iota.

Conversely, we waver like crazy in our other beliefs. For example, we may *say* we support our favorite sports team, but the second they miss a point in a play-off game, they become a "bunch of bums," and we're surfing for reruns of *Cupcake Wars*. We may *say* we believe in social causes like conservation and human rights, until it comes time to turn down *our* thermostat or crack open *our* checkbook for a donation. We may even *say* we believe in a supreme being, but the second anything goes wrong in our mismanaged lives, we rage at the heavens and shout, "Why? Why?" We question or even lose our faith.

No matter what Dog does, though, it's never enough to make us reject him or call our love for him into question. It's never enough to shake our faith.

The point is this: We profess to believe in all sorts of noble and worthy things, but we do not practice those beliefs consistently, day in, day out. On the other hand, Dogtologists practice their belief with absolute, unwavering commitment.

Over the centuries, Dogtology has become stronger with each generation.

III. Dog Is Fur Real

Why is our belief in Dog so much more powerful and unwavering than our other beliefs? It comes down to this: Most of our deep beliefs are abstract to us. And humankind is not very good at relating to abstractions. Abstractions, it turns out, are crap at catching balls and snuggling. Abstractions don't lick our face. Abstractions don't make us laugh after a long day of listening to Todd the interim regional sales manager explain the "Seven Cs of Successful Upselling." Abstractions aren't cute and fuzzy and they don't hog our beds.

We do much better with stuff we can see and feel and scratch.

When you think about it, the things we get from Dog every day are the very things we typically seek through spiritual or metaphysical belief:

- ❁ love
- ❁ unconditional acceptance
- ❁ non-judgment
- ❁ loyalty
- ❁ a feeling of partnership in life
- ❁ inspiration
- ❁ courage
- ❁ steadfastness
- ❁ joy

We *seek* these things through our belief systems, but, due to the *imperfection of our faith*, we don't always receive them.

We *unfailingly* get them from Dog, though.

So . . . maybe that was all part of the plan. Maybe Man and Dog were designed to be perfectly complementary partners here on Earth. Maybe it's Man's job to tame the elements, grow the food, build the houses, stitch the pockets to hold the treats, manufacture the tools, make the grocery lists, harness the energy, mow the lawns, watch the clocks, banish the fleas and ticks, clean up the poop, and drive the cars. And maybe it's Dog's role to teach Man how to love, play, run, live spontaneously, be a friend, and behave unselfishly. Oh, and find the scratch spot behind the ears.

Dog Saves

Man, because of his inherently weak faith, tends to doubt and blame the very almighty powers he strives so hard to believe in. But Dog is a being that Man can *always* trust in and never blame. So perhaps Dog came to Earth as Man's savior. After all, it wouldn't be the first time in history this sort of thing went down.

For Dogtologists, this is not a what-if. It is *the way things are.* Dogtologists may not have thought all of this stuff out in their heads, but they know it in their *bones.*

IV. The Ten Noble Qualities of Dog

Why canines? Of all the millions of flashy and exotic species that have graced this planet since Man arrived on the scene—lizards that walk on water, insects that glow with inner light, apes that mirror human emotions, beetles that can roll the most awesome dung-balls you've ever seen; really, you should check these things out—why is it that Dog alone has caught the enduring attention of Man? Why is it that Dog alone has become Man's universal companion, both in his home and in the world at large? (Cats share Man's home, too, but try taking one to the mall.)

Is it because dogs are helpful to us? Sure, dogs do a lot of practical jobs for us, but so do goats, oxen, lab rats, water buffalo, and reindeer. Is it because dogs are cute? Sure, they're cute, but so are kittens, chipmunks, piglets, ducklings, bunnies, canaries, meerkats, baby seals, pandas, and sea otters. Is it because dogs are docile? So are cows. Obedient? So are sheep. Smart? So are octopi. Humanlike? So are gorillas.

We love Dog for *all* of these qualities, but the reasons we *believe* in Dog and are uplifted by Dog go much, much deeper. When one ponders the true nature of Dog, one cannot help but conclude that, like our greatest saints and sages, Dog possesses truly noble qualities that the average person can only aspire to.

1. Dog Lives in the Moment

Dog exists in the *now*. Not in the five minutes ago. Not in the tomorrow. The *now*. Dog can make a rubber ball the center of his universe, but two seconds after the ball rolls away he forgets that it even existed and moves on to something else. Why? Because Dog does not live in his head. Man, on the other hand, is always somewhere else mentally: replaying the past, worrying about the future, fantasizing about the nonexistent, and forgetting all about that old Sunday school lesson, "Therefore do not worry about tomorrow, for tomorrow will worry about itself."

Dog is content wherever he finds himself, and never wishes to be elsewhere—well, except maybe on that walk Man keeps promising him. He doesn't find himself daydreaming about catching a Frisbee on the beach when he's chasing squirrels in the forest. Dog is simply *here*.

Dog interacts with the world fully and directly. He wouldn't log on to eHydrants.com to fake-spray a virtual mark or set up a virtual hook-up with another canine, nor would he watch other dogs play games on TV. No, he's out there in the world *doing* those things.

2. Dog Exudes Inner Light

Saints are often depicted with halos around their heads, which represent the "inner light" that special beings are said to exude, but no being on Earth exudes more "inner light" than Dog. A dog will never walk into a room of humans only to have them vaguely acknowledge his existence. When a dog walks into a room, everyone's attention immediately goes to him and stays there until he exits. Even at a church wedding, if a dog walks in and strolls down the aisle, who receives even more attention than the bride on her wedding day? You know who.

Dog exudes a light that lifts the human spirit and fills it with joy. In fact, dogs should have been created with halos. In the eyes of Dogtologists, they were.

3. Dog Is All-Knowing

Dogs are hyperaware of the world around them. With super-hearing and a sense of smell that is up to a million times stronger than Man's, Dog is able to process vastly more information about the world than humans are. Dog can simultaneously listen to an argument going on three houses away, locate the eight nearest sources of fresh meat, track the movements of twelve woodchucks chucking wood in the nearby forest, brace for the arrival of the mailman, and keep an eye on a toddler wandering near a swimming pool—all while busily gnawing on a fresh rawhide. Dog also has the uncanny ability to selectively hear. For some reason, Dog won't hear his name being yelled while he's rolling around in a fresh pile of *something* in the yard, but open a candy wrapper two miles away and watch him come running. Dog even knows when an earthquake is coming and, by some accounts, can tell when a human epileptic patient is about to experience a seizure and when humans have undiagnosed cancer in their bodies.

4. Dog Is Unconditionally Loving

Dog knows that humans are about as skilled at giving unconditional love as they are at playing underwater billiards. Dog will never respond with sarcasm after being shooed out of a room, or give the silent treatment when another dog eats his food in his absence. In fact, Dog's love is so unconditional that when a person locks his spouse *and* Dog in the trunk of the car for an hour, just watch and see when the trunk is opened which one comes running to Man first, licking and grinning.

Dog does not care if Man is rich or poor, young or old, a PhD or a dropout, drop-dead gorgeous or back-end-of-a-wildebeest ugly, because Dog loves Man so much his butt quakes with love and excitement. Man doesn't love *anything* enthusiastically enough to make his butt quake—Man is too busy holding back and punishing others for past mistakes—but Dog loves unconditionally and forgives endlessly. In fact, Dog's only question is, "Do you love me *now?*" Man takes the love of Dog for granted, but if Dog withheld his love and stopped talking to Man, Man would have to enter long-term therapy to explore why Dog shut him out.

5. Dog Is Humble and Free of Ego

Dog allows himself to be treated poorly, yet still loves. In fact, if Dog could, he would wash the feet of humans who treat him badly. Why?

Because Dog has no self-esteem? No. *Because Dog has no ego.* The surest hallmark of the spiritually evolved being is freedom from pride.

Dogs allow humans to clad them in pink ruffle dresses, call them names like Twinkle-Cakes, and stare openly at them as they empty their bowels. Dogs eat humans' crumbs off the floor and lick up their spills. Not because dogs are "lower" than humans, but because they are way past Man's ego games. And because they can.

If Dog ruled the world (officially) there would be no war. Or politics. Or comb-overs. Dog does not do comb-overs.

6. Dog Is Fiercely Loyal

Dog gives Man his absolute, utmost loyalty, at all times, unfailingly. Dog does not care whether Man is a criminal, an idiot, a failure, fat, skinny, brilliant, or mentally challenged. Dog does not care about what's in it for him by being Man's friend, because when Dog offers friendship, it is friendship for life.

Dog knows that humans are about as loyal as fleas during mating season, that they're more faithful to their hair-care products than they are to each other, and that half of their marriages end in divorce, yet Dog remains loyal, through thick and thin. Dog never fails Man!

7. Dog Is Joyous and Grateful

Dog is not a "glass half-empty" being. Dog does not grumble his way through life, failing to notice the garden of Eden he lives in or becoming animated only when the cable goes out for a minute or the Internet connection is a fraction of a second slower than expected.

While Man is about as spontaneously joyful as a barnacle, Dog constantly celebrates life. Dog is filled with more joy at the prospect of a walk in the woods than humans are at the birth of their children.

8. Dog Embraces Silence

Dog is at peace with himself and comfortable in silence. Dog does not need to make constant noise to validate his existence. To Man the thought of spending even a single minute alone, in silence, is more terrifying than the idea of inviting Leatherface over for nacho night. That's why Man fills every moment of his day with nervous chattering, humming, foot stomping, TV blasting, iTunes, video games, and YouTube. Dog, meanwhile, is simply "there."

Because Dog's hearing is far more sensitive than Man's and covers a wider frequency range, Man's constant noise is undoubtedly an unpleasant experience for Dog. For example, some of Man's machines, such as vacuum cleaners, emit sounds that can be quite painful to dogs, while some high-tech gadgets, such as digital alarm clocks, emit constant high-pitched signals that are too faint for humans to hear (so they aren't bothered) but sound like fire alarms to canines.

Dog does not woof, snarl, whine, scratch, and growl for hours on end every day, and then, when bored with that, turn on machines that play sounds of other dogs whining and barking. If Dog did things like that in the presence of humans, he would soon find himself living in an empty refrigerator box at the dump, making sad eyes to the tune of a Sarah McLachlan song.

9. Dog Is Selfless and Heroic

Scientists claim that animals are only capable of acting in ways that ensure their own survival, but that is probably because scientists haven't spent much time with Dog.

Since the dawn of history, dogs have been performing selfless acts of heroism, such as running into burning buildings to save Man, shielding Man from attacks by absorbing the blows themselves, and risking their lives to rescue lost or trapped humans. In fact, when the ruins of Pompeii were excavated, a dog was found frozen in the act of shielding a young boy's body. A tag around the dog's neck described three previous times the dog had saved the same boy's life.

Dog is a true hero. By contrast, Man throws the word "hero" around as if it's bargain-brand confetti and uses it to describe supermodels who lose fifteen pounds on the lemonade-purge diet.

Dog is unselfish in a way that Man can only aspire to be. True, human firefighters, police, and soldiers are heroic, but Dog gets no paycheck for being so, no health insurance plan, no trip to the Bahamas. Heroism is so yawningly standard for Dog, that Dog is lucky if Man remembers to toss him a Milk-Bone after he pulls a baby from a burning car. It's just what Dog does. No big.

10. Dog Heals

Some of the more spiritual members of the human race seem to have the mysterious ability to heal the sick, but there's little mystery about the way Dog does it—without even trying (heck, without even realizing it!). Dog even has chemicals in his saliva that contain antiseptic properties that speed the healing of wounds. In fact, it was Dog who licked the wounds of a guy named Lazarus, trying to apply a little first aid to the dude.

Dog can alleviate pain, reduce blood pressure, and even delay the symptoms of aging. The best Man can do is to try not to stand on a patient's oxygen hose when Dog shows up to heal with his mere presence.

V. Dogs in Religion

Historically speaking, the noble qualities of Dog were not immediately apparent to Man. It takes a while for big ideas to filter their way into the collective human psyche. When Copernicus first suggested that the earth revolves around the sun, for example, the science club kicked him out without refunding his dues. When the zero was first introduced as a math concept, it took centuries for the world to wrap its mind around it ("Uhhh . . . tell me again, how can *nothing* be *something*?"). Big ideas sink in slowly. Dogtology is another such big idea. It took many centuries to gain the momentum it now enjoys.

Scattered throughout history are examples of cultures and religions that were early adopters of Dogtological beliefs. The Nosarii of western Asia, for instance, worshipped a dog as their deity, and the Kalangs of Java had a "cult of the red dog." Dogs are still worshipped in Nepal at a festival called Khicha Puja. But the truth is, humankind has worshipped *lots* of other creatures, including goats, rodents, serpents, plants, and fish. So evidently, Man has not been too picky about what to bow down to.

What's more interesting are the historical cases that reveal the mindset of the worshippers themselves.

Egypt

It is clear that in ancient Egypt dogs were highly honored. After all, they were routinely eviscerated, embalmed, mummified, and entombed—which was the way those wacky ancient Egyptians said, "I love you."

Historians often claim that *cats* were more revered than dogs in ancient Egypt. As evidence, they point to the fanciful cat images seen in Egyptian art. Dogs, on the other hand, were usually portrayed more realistically (which meant, according to some researchers, that dogs were no big woof). But perhaps these historians got it wrong. Could they have failed to appreciate the role cartoon humor played in ancient Egypt, as evidenced by their cat art? Perhaps what the historians failed to grasp is that all of those cat-themed statues and hieroglyphics were the ancient equivalent of comic strips. And whom were those cat cartoons designed to entertain? Dogs, of course! What if ancient Egyptians loved their dogs so much that they wanted to amuse them by depicting their natural enemies in goofy ways? Ahh, you can almost hear an Alexandrian sculptor chuckling with his buddies over mugs of millet beer after a long day of enshrining dogs in a pharaoh's tomb:

"Guess what I made today during my lunch break?"

"I don't know. . . . Another priestess with a cat head?"

"No, a *lion* head this time! Tomorrow I'm putting a giant disk on its head and giving it, like, a totally serious expression on its face."

"The boss will kill you, bro—she doesn't like us using company equipment to screw around like that!"

India

A tale from ancient India suggests that the roots of Dogtology may have been flourishing in that culture, too. In this sacred story, Yudhisthira strikes off into the mountains in search of the chariot of the god Indra. On the way, a skinny stray dog befriends him—not Eukanuba-ad-model skinny, but rather starving, bedraggled skinny. Still, there's something about its eyes. . . . Together Yudhisthira and the dog traverse burning sands, jagged rocks, and lethal mud pits. The dog sticks by Yudhisthira through thick and thin. The two finally reach the peak they are seeking, and Indra's voice rings out:

"You have made it! Come, jump into my chariot and we shall fly to heaven."

As Yudhisthira and his dog take a step toward the chariot, Indra raises a hand.

"Sorry," Indra says. "No dogs allowed. Heavenly policy and all."

Yudhisthira says to Indra, "Yo, four-arms, if my dog can't get in, I don't want to join this country club."

"Stop!" cries Indra as Yudhisthira and his dog turn to walk away.

At this moment the dog transforms into its true shape: the great god Dharma, lord of correct living.

"You passed your final test," barks—er, *says*—Dharma. "You have proven that you deserve to enter the gates of heaven."

Pure, undiluted Dogtology.

Ancient Greece

The great philosopher Diogenes the Cynic was said to hold Dog in higher esteem than he did his fellow man. (The word "cynic" is actually derived from the Greek word for "doglike"—not, surprisingly enough, from the word for "one who follows American politics closely.") Diogenes was a curious chap. It is said that he tried to emulate dogs in his behavior and that he believed in eating from garbage heaps, relieving himself on trees, and howling at full moons. (He also masturbated in public, to which Dog reportedly responded, "Dude, if you're going to make a big point about emulating us, could you please not do *that*?") Diogenes is also said to have celebrated dogs as courageous guardians and models of morality.

Hard to get past the masturbating-in-public thing, though ...

VI. Evidence of Dogtology Around Us

The time has now come to openly celebrate our feelings and beliefs about Dog. The time has come to elevate Dogtology to a formal belief system that stands proudly alongside all the other great *-isms* and *-ologies* of the world. And that is exactly what is happening. The physical signs of Dogtology are spreading all around the globe. Just as humans canonize their saints, they also "canine-ize" their world. Here are just a few examples of Man's exuberant dog worship:

- dog images on signs and billboards
- a National Dog Day observance
- a constant stream of dog-themed books on bestseller lists (wag, wag!)
- mobile dog-grooming services with names like Waggin' Wheels, Pooch Patrol, and Dog-Gone Clean
- dog comic strips in newspaper and magazines
- dog-food and dog-medication advertisements accompanying nearly every mouse click made online
- dogs featured in ads for every *human* product from health insurance to erectile-dysfunction medication (is it possible to watch three consecutive TV commercials without seeing a dog in one of them?)

- talking dogs in movies, TV shows, and cartoons—and even dreams!

- *entire stores* with names like Pawsitively Yours, More Bones About It, Wags to Riches, and Necessary Ruffness, all devoted to dog merchandise

- dog plastic surgeons, dentists, and orthodontists

- entire dog departments in supermarkets and department stores

- YouTube videos of dogs doing random human acts, such as driving a lawn mower or reading a book

- backyards and homes designed entirely around dogs

- dog psychologists (because humans think they need one, so why not dogs, too?)

Humans tell themselves that dogs worship and adore them, but would dogs flock to a movie called *Marvin and Me*—about a dog and his boy? Would dogs make YouTube videos of *humans* catching Frisbees in their teeth? Would dogs open a salon called To Hair Is Human?

Humans don't just love dogs; they obsess over them. But, like the fish that can't see the water it's swimming in, humans aren't always aware of their obsession, because they're so immersed in it. An interesting experiment would be to substitute—overnight—a giant sloth for every image of Dog, reference to Dog, and instance of Dog devotion that exists in culture. One glance around such a world and humans would be looking at each other, scratching their heads and saying, "What the heck is our issue with sloths?" They would immediately shut down their businesses, go on a forty-day fast, and embark on an intense period of self-examination.

How did dog "worship" so thoroughly take over the world? Perhaps it's like the Internet. Once humans had it, it became an addiction. They could no longer live without it and had to have access to it everywhere. Similarly, Dog devotion just grew, one paw-print sticker at a time.

VII. History's Greatest Hookup

From what can be gathered from history, Dog has always enjoyed a unique relationship with Man. As just a few examples:

- Dogs were the first animals Man ever fed voluntarily. Man probably fed the saber-toothed cat now and then, but that was less about volunteerism and more about poor foot traction.

- Dogs were the first animals to share Man's domicile—at least on an invitational basis. (It was actually the rats and cockroaches that pioneered the concept of "*Mi casa es su casa*.")

- Dogs were the first animals ever to play with Man, not just as a chew toy.

- A dog, Laika (Russian for "Barker"), was the first animal in space.

- A canine is credited with saving and nurturing Romulus and Remus, who later founded the city of Rome.

So, how did Man and Dog first partner up? Science reveals that canines first encountered Man in the form of the gray wolf, and later evolved into the modern "domesticated" dog. How and when this change took place, however, no one knows for sure. The old theory was that Man plucked wolf puppies from the wild and raised them in captivity so they would be docile. (However, *how* Man managed to coax newborn pups away from their snarling she-wolf moms or *why* Man thought that sharing his living room with an apex predator was a good idea has never been adequately explained.)

Scientists are now starting to suspect that it was actually Dog that scoped out *Man* for partnership, rather than vice versa. That's right: Dog may have been the agent of *Man's* domestication, according to the Duke Canine Cognition Center. In fact, research reveals that early Dog had thoughts along the lines of the following:

- "Hmm, look at ol' Two Legs over there. He loves to hunt and gather almost as much as I love to eat. I wonder what it would take to sink my teeth into some of that yummy meat he collects. Maybe if I grin and act super friendly toward him . . ."

- "Hmm, ol' Knobby Knees has amazing paws. Maybe if I help him with his chores, he'll use them to do some work for me. Like make me a bed to sleep in. Or fill my water dish. Or throw me a ball."

- "Hmm, ol' Long Arms, Long Fingers seems to think I'm cute. Maybe if I play up the cuteness, he'll let me hang around inside his camp and share his warm fire on cold nights."

- "Hmm, when I make big eyes and tilt my head at ol' Fur Only In Strange Places, he doesn't seem to care if I do no work at all. In fact, he wants to do things for me."

Dog now lives in leisure, warmth, and comfort, while Man works fifty-some hours a week so he can feed, house, play with, and care for Dog (including giving him better medical care than Man gives his own human children). From an evolutionary perspective, then, which species is serving which?

What *is* known for sure is that as history has unfolded, Dog has climbed up the ladder to higher and higher roles in human society. Dog started out at the very bottom rung and now finds himself where he is today: catching z's, munching Pup-Peroni on the sofa, and waiting for the humans to come home from work so he can get his ears scratched.

VIII. The Changing Role of Dogs in Society

While there is room for interpretation and opinion, the progression of Dog's role in society probably went something like this.

Janitor

Dog's first role with Man was, essentially, "Cleanup on aisle five!" Many scientists believe that the relationship between Man and Dog first began when camps of human hunters would toss away perfectly good pancreases, gall bladders, and pituitary glands. Dog began tentatively approaching human camps and "cleaning up" after him. Humans soon realized that there were benefits to having Dog perform this janitorial service: less stench of death, fewer flies and rats, and a diminished chance of diseases caused by the parasites that fill rats' coats like clowns in a clown car. And so Man began to welcome Dog into his settlements. Man naturally began to like Dog, and Dog began to tolerate Man—even learning to endure the tired stories of his own heroism that Man repeated ad nauseam around the campfire.

Security Guard

Side benefits began to emerge from this arrangement. For example, Dog, with his superior senses, would sit up and bark whenever strange animals or humans were approaching the settlement. This would alert Man to potential predators, invading armies, and traveling loincloth salesmen. Man realized he was much safer when Dog was around. And Dog not only guarded Man's villages from attack at night, but also protected Man's crops from being raided by bunnies and hobbits and the like. (In fact, it is well known in dog circles that agriculture would not have evolved without Dog's protection.) Dog thus assumed the official role of guard, willing to protect Man night and day in exchange for a roof bearing a "Fido" sign over his head and a nicer cut of the meat at mealtimes. (Fido, BTW, simply meant "faithful" in Latin, a generic label for all dogs, not necessarily a proper name!)

Hunter

It didn't take too many millennia for Man to figure out that Dog's talents for hearing and smelling could be used for other purposes. And so Man began to take Dog on the hunt with him. It soon became clear who was the teacher and who was the student. Dog had more hunting talent in his left hind paw than Man had in his entire weak, nearly furless body. Dog taught Man how to hunt like a pack animal, how to flank, track, and isolate prey and avoid being trampled to pulp by roving bands of woolly mammoths.

Scapegoat

Man soon began to realize that there was another big perk to having Dog share his camp with him: Since Dog could not speak to explain his actions or defend himself ("Who chewed up the bear rug couch?!"), Dog could be conveniently blamed for practically any screw-up for which Man was responsible, including eating the leftover roasted elk leg, peeing on the chieftain's deerskin coat, or passing gas during the sacred tribal ceremony. Man owed Dog a tremendous debt of gratitude for Dog's playing the scapegoat (which Dog did not let Man forget when it came to bacon-slicing time).

Soldier

Man next began to grant Dog the "honor" of serving alongside him on the battlefield. While Dog did not quite understand why getting stabbed with pointy things was considered a good thing, he was willing to do his part for Man—as long as the gravy kept flowing. (However, Dog opted out of having medals pinned on his coat; one stabbing was enough.)

Employee

As Man began to recognize Dog's many talents and virtues, he then started to "adopt" dogs more and more into his community life. Man began assigning dogs civilian jobs right alongside humans. Dogs became shepherds, laborers, and pullers of sleds. Later, Man began to use search-and-rescue dogs to locate buried skiers who thought that surfing an avalanche would be gnarly fun. Dogs also rescued survivors of earthquakes and candlelit natural gas expeditions. Police dogs were able to track down and catch criminals even before they ditched their bandit masks. Bloodhounds could find missing children by taking one sniff of their Happy Meal toys. Detection dogs could sniff out bombs, drugs, illegal substances, and overripe kiwi fruit at airports. Cadaver dogs were able to locate lifeless bodies after natural disasters and four-day sales-training seminars.

Caretaker

The next logical step came when Man began "allowing" Dog to care for him in more direct and personal ways. This came in the form of mobility-assistance dogs, guide dogs, and hearing dogs. Therapy dogs began to help the sick, injured, and elderly to heal more quickly and stay healthy longer—simply by sitting there and exuding doggie goodness to the weaker human.

Pet

Throughout history there has been a steady progression toward that highly coveted role that has now thoroughly eclipsed all other doggie roles. This is, of course, the role of pet. Pet is an extremely elevated, almost deified, position in human life. As pet, a dog's role is to be taken care of, to be fed, to be housed, to be taken for walks, to be played with, and to be praised and admired. Pets are given their own food dishes, their own beds, and their own toy boxes. They go on vacations with the family and receive wrapped gifts on holidays. In return, pets are required to, um . . . to do, uh . . . well, absolutely nothing. Zilch. Nada. Zip. Except lie there and be cute—*if* they feel like it. As of the early 21st Century, there were four hundred million domesticated dogs on Earth, and the vast majority of these were pets.

Media Star

Of course, the very highest reverence Man accords another being is celebrity status—rock star, pro athlete, movie star. Not only did Dog begin to perform for Man in circuses, dog shows, and sporting events, but he also began to star in Man's books, films, and TV shows (and to utter timeless quotes like "Ruh-roh, Raggy, I rink I repped in romething ret"). Canine stars on the sidewalks of Hollywood Boulevard may one day outnumber human stars.

Confidant/Trusted Companion

For some dogs, the role of pet has evolved into an even higher position: that of sidekick, best friend, and confidant. Dogtologists today view their dogs on par with their spouses, children, and best friends. They give dogs their highest trust, deepest love, and fullest respect. For many humans, in fact, the relationship with their dog is the deepest one they have in their lives (and many of these folks, sadly, are married with children).

Dog's evolving relationship with Man has finally reached its logical conclusion. *We* now serve *Dog*, not the other way around.

IX. Believers and Nonbelievers

As we celebrate the continuing emergence of Dogtology on Earth, we must become sensitive to the many types of believer that exist. Dogtology, like most belief systems, has followers at every level, and we must be respectful and tolerant of all of them. There are fledgling Dogtologists, diehard Dogtologists, and, let's face it, fanatics as well. Fanatics form the "radical sect" of Dogtologists known as Dog Show People, who spend every weekend cramming their pups into their minivans and traveling to places like the Blatz Beer Expo Center in Milwaukee, Wisconsin, to rub shoulders with fellow Dog Show People.

But no Dogtologist should judge another! There's room for all within the fold!

DUDs

Which brings us, of course, to the subject of DUDs.

A DUD (Doesn't Understand Dogtology) is a person who just doesn't get it, didn't receive the memo, feels no connection to dogs, and doesn't understand what all the fuss is about. DUDs come in many different types. Some DUDs support Dogtology in their loved ones but don't practice it themselves. Others actively dislike or fear dogs. To Dogtologists, this is incomprehensible; it's kind of like saying, "I don't like air—just never cared for it very much." But remember, most DUDs are simply lost souls who have not yet seen the light or who have had a bad dog experience as a child that has kept them from opening their hearts to Dog. None of us has the right to judge a DUD or to feel superior to a DUD (though we do, since we know they are wrong). Nor do we have an obligation to try to convert DUDs into practicing Dogtologists.

The good news is that DUDs are curable. Well, most are. But preaching is not the way to effect a cure. What's needed is quality time spent with a dog. You just have to trust that this will happen in its own time and resist the temptation to proselytize or interfere.

DUDs can sometimes be spotted because of the words they speak. Be sure you are in a safe place before reading the following statements (they are not for the weak of heart):

- "Dog" is sometimes used to refer to an ugly person.
- "In the doghouse" means to be in trouble.
- "Dogging it" means not trying.
- "Dog eat dog" means everyone out for himself.
- "Dog days" refers to a period of stagnation or uncomfortable heat.
- "Throw to the dogs" means to heartlessly abandon someone.
- "Dog tired" means absolute exhaustion.
- "Dog meat" means you are finished.

A DUD might also use the phrases "sick as a dog," "dirty dog," "dog's chance," "call off the dogs," "work like a dog," "wouldn't wish that on a dog," "hair of the dog that bit me," "meaner than a junkyard dog," and "if you lie down with dogs, you'll wake up with fleas."

Why these negative connotations about Dog? Why do humans feel warmed, awed, inspired, and healed by dogs on one hand, yet feel superior to them on the other? Maybe it's because, deep down, humans sense Dog's superiority, and their egos are threatened by it. So they resort to that good ol' schoolyard trick, the verbal put-down. Think about it. Which kid got the most grief in grammar school? The brainiac, of course. Who is the butt of all the snide remarks around the company water cooler? The rising young office superstar, of course. Whom do broke, miserable souls with shattered dreams love to make fun of? The rich and famous, of course. (That's the whole reason tabloids exist!)

Believers in Dogtology don't fall into that trap, as a rule. Dogtologists are unabashed in their veneration of Dog. And that's really the point of this way of life—to come out of the closet about that deep and abiding reverence for Dog.

x. The Ten Commands of Dog

What, then, does it mean to be a practicing Dogtologist? What are the hallmarks of our belief system? Fortunately, we have not been left alone in our quest for answers. Dog, in his infinite wisdom, has left some guidance behind for us to follow. It comes in the form of the Ten Commands. The Ten Commands are the fundamental "dog-ma" of Dogtology. (There is also the Eleventh Command, which can only be found in the lost Book of Fleas, a book usually considered apocrypha in Dogtology. Folklore tells us that it was lost in the Great Flea Bath of 519 AD—After Dog. The search for the lost Book of Fleas has been gaining momentum during the 20th and 21st centuries.)

When Dog created the Ten Commands and *how*, exactly, Man came to possess them are questions shrouded in mystery. In one version of the legend, a farmer in northeastern Quebec was plowing his fields when he saw a bush burning at the edge of a dry cornfield. He tried to put out the fire but couldn't find any water. Suddenly a giant Irish wolfhound appeared from within the cornrows, strolled up to the bush, and peed on it. The dog then disappeared into the corn, never to be seen again. When the farmer examined the charred remains of the bush, he found two sacred stone tablets waiting there, wet, but none the worse for the wear. In another version of the myth, the great Native American trickster god, Coyote, cracked the tablets over the head of an old Crow chieftain who accidentally kicked a puppy sleeping outside his teepee.

Whatever the folklore, the important thing to know is that the Ten Commands are for our enlightenment. They are so profound, however, that we must digest them one command at a time. Here is the first.

And Dog said unto Man:

> FIRST COMMAND
>
> THOU SHALT NOT ALLOW MORE THAN SEVEN CONSECUTIVE SECONDS TO PASS WITHOUT CALLING THY DOG "GOOD," "CUTE," OR "SMART," AS IF IT WERE BRAND NEW INFORMATION.

The important thing to remember is that Dogtology, at its core, is much more than a dog-matic set of beliefs and practices; it is a state of mind. It's the *place one lives*, where one recognizes and acknowledges one's adoration for Dog and the privilege of sharing one's life with Dog. Stripped to its bare bones (mmm, bones), Dogtology is that and nothing more. (Except maybe a pair of foam antlers at Christmas time.)

THE BOOK OF LEASHES

Man's Attachment to Dog—Emotionally, Mentally, Spiritually, and Literally

I. The Leash

Behold the leash: a simple, flexible cord that links a dog on one end to a human on the other. Elegantly uncomplicated. And yet no object holds more layers of meaning in the world of Dog and Man. Guilt and joy, domination and liberation, soul care and bladder care—all woven together in a few feet of nylon braid.

History reveals that Man and Dog have been binding themselves to one another via the leash for millennia. Mosaics from ancient Pompeii show dogs wearing chain leashes. An ancient Greek carving depicts two toga-draped fellows checking out each other's abs as they conduct the familiar meet-and-greet with two dogs on leashes. A controversial Egyptian hieroglyphic seems to show a slave holding a dog on a leash, while he surreptitiously toe-flips a dog doo into a nearby papyrus bush.

Wherever Dog and Man are found together, there is usually a leash involved (at least there should be, according to municipal codes).

II. Unleashing the Leash's Symbolism

As a device, the leash couldn't be simpler. Throughout history, leashes have been made from a variety of materials: hemp, chain, leather, nylon braid, and pig intestine (which, as was ruefully discovered by the holder of the patent for the device, turned out to be a favorite doggie snack).

There are short "tab" leashes, used for training and competition; there are long, retractable leashes to give travel distance to the dog and fishing reel–style control to the dog walker. There are leashes designed to attach to bicycles (slow-moving bicycles, at least). And there was also the ill-conceived "locomotive leash" (which was designed to attach to the back end of a train's caboose and was quickly outlawed after a regrettable incident). The leash has been so successful that humans now use it for a variety of non-canine purposes, such as ensuring that the correct surfer's body is tethered to the correct surfboard after a mass wipeout, and for dragging uncooperative toddlers across the floor of the Piggly Wiggly.

When used with a dog, the leash can symbolize fun, exercise, recreation, and bonding. But it can also symbolize hard work, obedience training, and transportation to an undesirable location, such as the vet, the groomer, the kennel, or Outside Where the Rain and Thunder Live. Whenever the human reaches for the leash, a dog must quickly assess whether the appropriate reaction would be to jump with joy or retreat under the table (where no one can ever possibly find him).

III. The Traditional View of the Leash

No object more clearly draws the line between the mindset of traditional dog "owners" and that of Dogtologists than the leash. In the view of traditionalists (i.e., those who still believe humans can "own" and "control" Dog), the leash represents the following:

Mastership. The leash symbolizes the master-subject relationship that traditional dog "owners" believe they have with their dogs. The master stands tall and erect, in the dominant position, while the subject crouches at his feet. The master holds the "controlling" end of the leash, with the subject attached to the "controlled" end. The question of who winds up carrying whose poop in a warm plastic bag is conveniently glossed over.

Restraint. The leash is viewed as a means of restraint, of breaking the dog's spirit. Without the leash, the dog's primitive instincts would

presumably run wild. Humans, on the other hand, believe they possess a wondrous faculty called "self-control" that allows them to govern their base impulses *without* a leash. This faculty, of course, works about as well as screen doors on a submarine.

Obedience and control. The leash symbolizes human control over dogs' behavior. Humans use the leash to parade their canines at dog shows and to harness their work services. When used properly, the leash is meant to keep the dog in the submissive "heel" position. But because a leash is made of fabric instead of titanium clamps, it is more common to see the dog running ahead of the human, with the human flying behind the dog like a screaming kite made of meat.

Lawfulness. The leash also symbolizes humans' desire to control dogs on a societal level. The leash law is a popular piece of legislation that allegedly protects humans from the dangerous rebel nation of Dog. Leash laws stipulate where and when a dog may be allowed to run free (i.e., nowhere and never, except on the human's private property or the elusive dog park). Leash laws create the illusion that humans are safer than they were a few decades ago when dogs were allowed to roam free. (What humans tend to forget about the pre-leash-law days is the joy they used to feel when local dog friends would drop by the yard for a visit; the spontaneous help they would get from dogs who were free to do things like rescue humans from fires; and, of course, the fun they'd have playing "Guess the Dad" whenever a female dog became pregnant.)

IV. Dogtology: A More Enlightened View of the Leash

Dogtologists tend to view the leash a little differently. While they recognize that the leash is often a necessary management device (for the humans), they know the real reason the leash was invented: to stop their dogs from running away.

Beneath all of the posturing about control and mastery, humans are deeply insecure about their dogs' love. So they literally handcuff themselves to their dog. When it comes to dogs, humans are not ready to embrace the "if you love somebody, set them free" philosophy. Man is afraid that if he sets his dog free, the dog will run off and live with the Feinsteins down the street. Or that it will join a little doggie commune in the woods, where canines run around in packs at all hours of the night and taste things that ought never be put in the mouth.

And so humans create an elaborate system of laws, fences, and leashes to keep dogs restrained. In Dogtology, the leash is the ultimate symbol not of Man's domination of Dog, but of Man's need to be Super Glued to Dog. Humans pretend the leash is there because they want to safeguard their world against dog bites, dog deposits, and dog pregnancies. Ah, but deep down, it's all about Man's attachment to his canine partner.

V. Separation Anxiety

One way humans deal with their attachment to Dog is by choosing to believe that the dog suffers from separation anxiety. Humans make a huge deal about leaving their dogs home alone for a few hours or about boarding them in a kennel for a few days. Dogtologists even get anxious about leaving the dog in the car for three minutes while they run into a 7-Eleven to buy lotto tickets and a Slurpee (nervously holding up the just-a-sec finger to the dog as they dash into the store).

In order to help ease Dog's supposed separation anxiety, humans do things like leave the television on "for them" when they go out for the evening, or leave a shirt with the human's scent on it in the dog's bed. (Yes, humans do this.) When they're going to be away for more than a day, some Dogtologists actually call and talk to their dog at the doggie hotel or at home. Many Dogtologists, though they hate to admit it, have even talked to their dog via the answering machine.

Who really misses whom? Are dogs really in a panic when humans leave them? The short answer is no (well, maybe for a little while—but not for long). Nope, the dog will plop down with its chin on the floor and let out a rumble of contentment, trying to decide where to start the hunt for something to eat. It may be more accurate to say that dogs might not miss Man so terribly when Man is gone, but they can feel *Man* missing *them*; humans are the ones who become anxious and neurotic when they're away from their dogs. That might explain why dogs follow humans around as if they're made of cheese when they see them packing a suitcase, or wail like Greek funeral mourners when humans go to work. The dog's heart is breaking *for the human* because the dog wonders if the human will be able to get along without it.

Because humans rank themselves as the top-dog species, though, they tend to view the anxiety as coming from the pup. But in most cases it's *their own* anxiety and loneliness that humans are sensing. When the dog is at the groomer's, it's the human who senses a deafening silence in the house. When the human goes to work, it's the human who needs to have her pup's pictures on her iPhone so she won't have to go eight whole minutes without seeing Coco's face. When the human goes to a party at night, it's the human who starts itching to get home by eleven. Because the dog needs to pee? Sure, if you say so.

VI. Man's Loyal Companion

Loyalty is a different animal than attachment. Man is attached to Dog; Dog is loyal to Man.

Attachment is based on need. That is, the attach*er* feels a strong emotional need for the attach*ee*. A certain amount of attachment between humans is necessary and healthy, of course, especially during their developmental years. Infants who form attachments to loving, attentive caregivers, for example, grow up to be healthy, stable adults. Conversely, babies who form attachments to twirling plastic clown mobiles grow up to be adults who are inordinately attracted to shiny objects and display a stunning mastery of one-syllable words. But a little attachment goes a long way. Just ask Norman Bates's mom.

Loyalty, on the other hand, is based on *choice*, not need. It is a noble choice.

Loyalty is the commitment to stand by someone regardless of how difficult and inconvenient it is when that someone does something really awful. Like when your best friend finally returns your DVD copy of *Best In Show* and you discover they had used it as a coaster.

VII. Hooked on Dog

Humans become uncomfortable when their dog spends too much time away from them in another part of the house. Humans call out to the dog, telling themselves that the object of their affection needs a little face time with them. And if the dog doesn't come when the human calls, the human will actually bribe the dog for affection.

"Come on, Patches. Come see Daddy and he'll give you a treat!"

When bribing doesn't work, the human goes to the dog, gets down on the floor, and nuzzles him. "Oh, look at you, you poor thing. All alone out here in the kitchen."

Right. Poor thing. Busy eyeballing the cookie jar way up there on that shelf and calculating distances and dimensions of climbing surfaces when the human came in and ruined it all.

Humans seek out dog-friendly vacation spots, dog-friendly outdoor restaurants, dog-friendly hotels. They invented Bring Your Dog to Work Day and Dog Happy Hour. In the absence of their dogs, devoted Dogtologists can experience actual withdrawal symptoms, such as anxiety, increased illness, and depression. When these devotees are away from their dogs, they talk about their dogs, shop for their dogs, and imprint photos of their dogs on their coffee mugs.

Dogtologists, in fact, can actually smother a dog with attention. Out of an abundance of love and patience, a dog may allow the smothering to occur, but in reality will probably be thinking something like, *Jeez Louise, Mom, could you back off just a hair and let me finish this slightly used cupcake wrapper I found on the kitchen floor?!*

Some believers have experienced a situation where they were snuggling with their dog and it got up and wandered to the far end of the couch or the opposite side of the room. This is not because the dog is about to do a little off-gassing and wants to spare the human a nasal assault. It's because the dog just needs some "me time." In fact, when humans go out for the evening, dogs probably let out a sigh of relief, sort of like what humans do when a teenager goes to the mall for a couple of hours. *Finally! I thought they'd never leave! Ahh, I get the place all to myself for a little while. Now, where's that mystery turd I spotted in the basement last week?*

The fact is, dogs provide the emotional pulse of the house and humans don't know how to handle it when they're gone. Couples get nervous when they don't have the dog around as their relationship buffer. After all, without the dog to talk to in a moronic, high-pitched voice, they might have to talk to *each other*. AAAAAAGH! Family members twiddle their thumbs and look at their watches when they are forced to spend "quality family time" together without the dog.

VIII. A Measure of Attachment

Just how attached are humans to their dogs? There are ways to measure that attachment objectively. One measure is the way humans spend money. For the past several decades, humans have been spending a greater and greater percentage of their income on dogs. It's not just the *amount* they're spending (more than the gross national products of Kenya, Bolivia, Iceland, and New Guinea combined, BTW) but also the *ways* they're spending that money.

For the early part of the twentieth century, doggie spending was focused on things like dog food and basic dog equipment and on acquiring dogs. A couple of decades ago, though, humans began spending more on extras, such as dog grooming, "I Woof You" doggie T-shirts, and doggie wine-and-cheese gift baskets from Yappy Hour Vineyards. Humans started wanting to make their dogs both prettier and happier, and to qualify them to receive little report cards from the groomer that say things like, "I was a little angel. A+!"

Recently, another area where humans have increased their spending has been health care. Medical care for dogs has been expanding dramatically. Only a generation or two ago, when a dog had a serious illness, Pa would announce to the young'uns, "Hey, kee-ids, Smokey's gonna go stay with his cousins off in Flagstaff for a li'l while," then grab the old shotgun off the rack over the stove and take Smokey for one last ride in the pickup.

Today, we provide dogs with radiation, chemotherapy, stem cell therapy, genetic testing, and an array of surgical procedures that put dog care on par with human care. (Okay, true believers know that dog health care actually far *surpasses* human health care—something the DUDs would rise up in revolt about if they found out.) Truth is, humans are spending thousands of dollars per year on their dogs' medical care. In fact, they'd sooner cut their clothing budget and run around wrapped in taped-together Swiffers than cut back on health-care spending for their pooch. It would throw a Dogtologist into a tailspin if they were told they had to choose between taking Grandpa to the doctor or Smokey to the vet. One can almost hear Pa saying, as he grabs the shotgun off the rack, "Kee-ids . . . Grandpa's gonna go to live with his cousins in Flagstaff for a li'l while. . . ."

There has also been a sharp increase lately in mental health care for dogs. Only a few years ago, filmmakers could get an easy laugh by showing a dog visiting a shrink. Nowadays, in trendy dog parks across the country, it's not unusual to hear a surprised dog owner say to a friend, "So your dog's *not* in therapy?"

IX. The Walk

Human/canine attachment is best illustrated through the Walk.

The Walk is the centerpiece of all human/dog relationships. It is the part of the day around which all other parts revolve and that both dogs and their humans anticipate eagerly, though perhaps for different reasons. The Walk is the central and primary focus of Dogtologists.

The Walk is practiced in a wide variety of ways. Some humans see the Walk as an opportunity to practice discipline with their dogs. They require the dog to walk at "heel" position, to exhibit humanlike indifference to other humans and dogs, and to urinate only when and where permitted. For other humans the *dog* leads the way on the Walk and the human is dragged along like a tin can from a wedding-day limo. Some humans take their dogs for long, brisk walks that provide a full cardio workout; others take their dogs on brief, leisurely strolls that provide about as much exercise as lifting a plastic fork. Some humans talk to their dogs during the Walk; others talk to their Bluetooths; others talk to the voices in their heads (hard to distinguish from the Bluetooth users). Some humans allow their dogs to run free of the leash; others choke up on the leash as if they were marching their dogs into federal court on a perp walk.

There are even those dog-owning DUDs who *hire others* to walk their dogs. Dog-walking, in fact, has become one of the fastest-growing small businesses. But that's like hiring someone to go to church for you on Sunday or to sleep with your lover. It kind of misses the point.

And what *is* the point? The point is that the Walk is really for *the human*. It is the sacred time of day when Dogtologists get to spend time with their dogs, away from other pseudo-priorities. It gives the Dogtologist a sense of fulfillment and accomplishment. It is the time, each day, that Dogtologists get to openly celebrate their attachment to Dog.

Dogtological Guilt

Sadly for many of us, "celebration" is not in our vocabulary. And so we rely on guilt to motivate us to walk our dogs. This is particularly true for those of us who were raised in two of the world's other major religions—out of respect the names won't be mentioned here (though they rhyme with Shmatholicism and Shmudaism), but you know who you are. In those great traditions, the faithful are often served their moral lessons with a heaping helping of guilt to aid in the digestive process. Dogtologists are not to be outdone in the guilt department, however. Many Dogtologists elevate guilt to a higher art form than even the most devoted self-flagellator or sackcloth-wearer.

We often claim that dogs "make" us feel guilty when we don't take them for walks. We also say they "make" us feel guilty when we buy them off-price dog food, leave them home alone, forget to buy them birthday presents, tell them to get off the couch, or yell at them for mating with the legs of houseguests. We project a sense of hurt feelings onto the dog, claiming they are looking at us with sad eyes or "not speaking to us."

Actually, they're not doing anything *to* us, any more than Wilson the volleyball was "lecturing" Tom Hanks in *Cast Away*. *We* create all the guilt ourselves. Guilt, according to that infallible repository of all human knowledge, Wikipedia, "is a cognitive or an emotional experience that occurs when a person realizes or believes—accurately or not—that he or she has compromised . . . a moral standard."

Note that the definition includes no mechanism for canine sad eyes surgically implanting guilt into our souls. Guilt is entirely self-inflicted. The simple truth is that we feel guilty when we treat our dogs shabbily because we are emotionally attached to them and we fear doing anything that might weaken that emotional attachment.

In truth, dogs have learned to have very low expectations of us, so we don't hurt their feelings as easily as we think. They don't really *expect* us to treat them with dignity, loyalty, and honor—they know us too well—so they're not quick to withdraw from us or punish us when we screw up. Kind of like when a five-year-old calls *us* a "big fat stupid-head"; we consider the source. And when humans *do* hurt dogs, the power of dogs to forgive is so enormous and immediate we sometimes mistake it for forgetfulness. (Dog's power of forgiveness is second to One.) All of our self-flagellation comes from within. Dogs accept us and forgive us as the flawed species we are.

x. Dog Attachment for Fun and Profit

Writers, advertisers, and movie producers all know that the easiest way to manipulate human emotions (hence, human spending) is through their attachment to dogs. For example, is Target a pet store? No. Then why does Target use a dog named Bullseye as its mascot? The same reason RCA Victor used a dog named Nipper. Or why Nestlé used a dog named Farfel to sell powdered cocoa mix in the sixties. Remember Spuds MacKenzie and Budweiser beer? Taco Bell's Gidget the Chihuahua? Or what about Ubu Productions' tagline, "Sit, Ubu, sit. . . . Good dog," which somehow became an assurance of quality television programming? Why did Flying A use a basset hound named Axelrod to sell gasoline—because nothing says "quality refined-petroleum products" like a basset hound sitting in a doghouse? No. It's all because humans love dogs, and it doesn't matter one dog-hair that dogs are irrelevant to the products their images are plastered all over.

The film industry is keen on the power of Dog, too. Look at *The Artist*. The producers knew that the only way to lure moviegoers into paying full price for a film that didn't even have sound was to throw in a dancing dog. Without Uggie, they wouldn't have even recouped production and marketing costs.

XI. The Flipside: Attachment Can Backfire

To whip up nonstop nail-biting angst in a movie audience, just separate a dog from its family. *Lassie Come Home, Far from Home*, and *The Incredible Journey* created more heart problems than all the fake-butter popcorn ever consumed in movie theaters.

And of course, the pièce de résistance of heartbreaking in any work of fiction is to (hold your breath) have the dog die in the end. *Marley and Me, Old Yeller, Sounder, A Dog of Flanders, I Am Legend, My Dog Skip*, and *Turner and Hooch* each generated more therapy bills on their opening weekends than *Bambi* has in almost seventy-five years. Harming dogs in movies can be a very risky business, though. Many Dogtologists won't see a movie if they know a dog dies in it. Savvy filmmakers (whether Dogtologists or DUDs) know that if they're planning to make anything but the tearjerker of the century, they'd better follow this next command to the letter:

SECOND COMMAND

THOU SHALT NOT KILL THE DOG IN THE MOVIE.

Nuns can be maimed, elderly grocers run over in the street, star-struck young lovers and grizzled action heroes shot to pieces; resorts, villages, cities, and entire nations can be bathed in meteors, tidal waves, and diseases or besieged by alien armed forces from a distant galaxy. But *kill the dog* and prepare to hand out ticket refunds to enraged hordes of pigtailed little girls as they commence to take the Bijou theater down brick by brick, screaming at the imagined producers, "Die, you heartless bastards!"

The adult Dogtologist will promptly hire an attorney and sue for emotional distress, while taking time off work.

XII. Doggie Dependence

The myth Man tells himself is that Dog depends on *him*. That's an easy story to sell to humans. After all, Man provides Dog's food, water, shelter, and medical care. Man gives Dog his entertainment and exercise. Man graces Dog with his constant companionship. Therefore, obviously, Dog *needs* Man. . . . Right? Well, if that's true, then it seems strange that humans are the ones who are so obsessed with locking dogs in pens and tying them down. But if Dog *needs* Man so much, then humans shouldn't have to *force* dogs to hang around with them.

So maybe the reality is more like this. . . .

What's in It for Dog

There's no doubt that Dog derives certain *benefits* from sharing his life with Man:

* Man cooks.

* Man plans ahead. (Dogs, face it, would jump onto a runaway hot-air balloon to retrieve a Hot Pocket and would be halfway to Istanbul before thinking, *Maybe this wasn't such a great idea.*)

* Man has hands. Those things give awesome belly rubs!

* Man has pockets (wherein treats reside).

* Man creates the most amazing living quarters. Heat! Fridges! George Foreman Grills! Bring it!

* Man goes to the store and comes back with meat.

* Man likes to wrestle.

- Man can make an endless supply of clean water appear from metal pipes.
- Man pulls the ticks off the skin.
- Man praises and admires Dog, nonstop.
- Man drives cars for dogs to ride around in.

In short, Man does a host of jobs that are tricky for a quadruped without opposable thumbs. Still, partnering with Man is not the nonstop orgy of joy it may sound like. In fact, there are several disadvantages for Dog in the deal:

- Man talks.
- When Man isn't talking, Man turns on machines that talk.
- Man washes the hard-earned dead-rodent scent from Dog's coat and says, "Don't you smell pretty now?"
- Man talks.
- Man believes the terms "kibble" and "great meaty taste" can be used together in the same sentence.
- Man talks.
- Man's nose is about as sensitive as a cave troll is cuddly, so he has no idea how to share in Dog's experience of the world.
- Man talks.
- Man doesn't *get* the whole barking thing—he just misses the point entirely.
- Man talks.
- Man wakes his dog up whenever he feels like it, but gets really peeved when the dog does the same to him.
- Man talks.
- And talks.
- And talks.

So, it's quite possible that some dogs are not 100 percent on board with this living-with-Man thing. Many dogs, in fact, may often be a heartbeat away from saying *Listen, pal, screw this* and taking their chances out in the wild. Which is maybe why, every now and then, a human will open a door and a dog will just bolt out in a flash, like a streaker across the field at a football game. Sometimes the dog will come back a few hours later; sometimes the dog will head to Zihuatanejo and open a little tourist kennel with his old dog-pound buddy, never to be seen again.

When a dog runs away, it's the *human* who is crushed and distraught. You don't tend to see desperation on the face of the emancipated dog. No, there you see the look of a POW who, disguised as a mailbox, has just successfully tiptoed past the guard gate. A dog knows that he *can* walk away whenever he wants. He just chooses not to. Most of the time, anyway.

THIRD COMMAND

IF THY DOG RUNNETH AWAY, AND THOU HAST EXHAUSTED ALL OTHER MEASURES OF LURING HIM HOME, THOU SHALT RESORT TO THE ULTIMATE ACT OF DESPERATION: THE FOUR-WHEEL BRIBE.

THE FOUR-WHEEL BRIBE: A ritual by which the human, after failing to recover a runaway dog by setting out a trail of treats, screaming the dog's name until rupturing the larynx, and chasing the dog for hours on foot, must resort to tracking the dog by car, with the promise of giving the dog a ride. When the dog is ultimately duped into the car with a piece of cheese, the human must then fulfill his promise by providing the dog a minimum ten-minute car ride with its head out the window (even at 2:30 a.m.). Otherwise the Four-Wheel Bribe will fail to work in the future.

Man's Dependence on Dog

Humans, on the other hand, have always depended on dogs for countless things. History seems to indicate this. Without bloodhounds, Man would not be able to apprehend serial killers. Without herding-dogs, Man would have no wool. Without sled dogs, entire arctic civilizations would not have flourished. Ask a person with a seeing-eye dog or service dog how much they depend on their dog. Ask a soldier in battle whether his mine-sniffing dog is of much help.

Imagine, if you will, using other animals to perform certain roles:

* a seeing-eye cat
* a guide porcupine
* a mine-hunting hippo
* a crime-solving sheep
* a ministry badger
* a therapy goat
* a rescue gerbil

As is plain to see, Man depends on Dog. Thoroughly and completely. Case closed. Next topic.

XIII. CEO: Canine Executive Officer

While humans *officially* depend on Dog to serve all of the functions previously mentioned, and more, they unofficially depend on Dog to fill the most crucial role of all in a human household: CEO (Canine Executive Officer). As CEO, it is the dog's job to run the home, plain and simple. The role of Canine Executive Officer is similar to the role of a human CEO in a corporation. That is, motivating and delegating, but little of the actual work. In fact, if a human CEO is doing a flawless job, the company should be able to run itself in his or her absence; the CEO should be able to phone it in from the back nine. So it is with the canine CEO. The Canine Executive Officer barely lifts a paw and yet his family cannot function without him.

Here are some of the important corporate functions the Canine Executive Officer performs:

Providing structure. The CEO provides the daily activity structure for the team. From the dog's first feeding and peeing requirements of the day, through play time, training time, snuggle time, and walk time, to the end-of-day peeing and bedding rituals, the CEO ensures that the team's entire daily work schedule revolves around him.

Settling intra-team conflict. Humans do not like to fight in front of the dog, and when they do fight, they make amends by talking to the dog and through the dog. Countless marriages have been saved by the passive intervention of a dog. The CEO simply lies on the floor, while the conflicted parties test the communications waters by making inane vocalizations at each other and attributing them to the dog.

Motivating the team to work hard. Because of the high costs of retaining a CEO (food, medicine, training, grooming, high-level veterinary care, toys, equipment, treats, and so forth), which frequently exceed those of all other family members combined, the team remains highly motivated to earn income.

Prioritizing the allocation of resources. The CEO dictates the family's financial priorities. Planning a summer vacation? Not if the CEO needs orthopedic surgery.

Creating team unity. While most family members can't even agree on which flavor of ice cream to buy and are frequently seen arguing with one another about who gets to sit in the front seat of the car, they can always agree on making Dog happy.

Providing teachable moments for the team. With only themselves as behavioral examples, humans would be incapable of teaching children morality or character lessons. Dog's higher traits are required for this. The CEO provides endless living examples of loyalty, trust, friendship, love, and courage, which are, essentially, foreign concepts to the average human.

This harkens to the higher aspects of Dog. . . .

XIV. Canine Nonattachment

In spiritual circles, it has long been known that an air of detached liberation is the truest sign of an enlightened being. Dogs are the very essence of spiritual nonattachment. They are unattached to things, unattached to circumstances, and unattached to memories of the past or worries about the future. In other words, they have "arrived."

For example, when a dog loses a leg in a car accident, does it go into long-term psychotherapy? Does it mope and whine about its future career prospects? Does it join a support group for dog survivors of leg loss? No. It starts running around the yard and enjoying life as Tripod, the three-legged dog. Or, when a dog's puppies leave home, do the parents develop empty nest syndrome? Do they phone the puppies' new homes every couple of days and ask why the puppies never call? Hardly. Instead, a dog is more like *Hey there, sailor* to the very next canine stud that wanders into its yard to pee.

It's obvious: Dog is here to teach Man lessons of nonattachment. Sounds nuts? Then chew on this: *Why does Dog only seem to destroy things Man cares about the most?*

❧ Of either rug to pee on—the cashmere one costing three grand or the threadbare indoor/outdoor carpet in the kids' playroom—the dog will choose the cashmere, every single time.

❖ Of all the possible envelopes to turn into chew toys, the dog will always find the one containing the only existing photo of the wife's mother, or the deed to the husband's great-grandfather's gold mine, or the cash for that rare 1968 Boss 302 Mustang the son found on the Internet.

❖ Of all the possible times to misbehave, the dog will patiently wait until Thanksgiving Day, when there are twenty-seven guests in the home, to decide something like, *You know what I'm getting tired of? The "No Stealing Meat from the Table" rule around here.*

❖ Of all the shoes to vomit on, Dog will choose the $1,500 Giuseppe Zanotti jeweled loafer belonging to a dinner guest. Yet, the human is thankful that at least the pooch didn't decide to *eat* the shoe.

Does Dog do these things because it wants to make Man angry? Dog does not have that kind of meanness in him. He chews up, barfs on, and pees all over the things Man is most attached to not only because he can, but simply because he wants Man to realize, "Hey, take a chill pill. . . . It's only *stuff.*"

Truth is, while someone might stay angry for weeks at someone who deliberately destroys his favorite things, Man can't stay mad at a dog for more than five minutes. Before long, the human is rolling on the floor with that dog, laughing and playing games again.

And that was Dog's whole point. It's only stuff.

XV. The Yoga of the Leash

So, what about *Dog's* attitude toward that timeless object, the leash? Is it not possible that Dog, in his wisdom, recognizes Man's insecurity about Dog's love? If that's true, then perhaps Dog permits himself to be leashed to Man as an ultimate act of compassion. Perhaps Dog views the leash as the ultimate lifeline yoking him to Man.

In Eastern philosophy, the term "yoga" means "to yoke." That is, to yoke the realm of the spirit to the realm of the body. In Dogtology, then, the leash becomes the ultimate yogic device, a sacred object that yokes the human to the canine. Via the leash, the human is able to achieve oneness with Dog.

This makes perfect sense if one looks at where the leash is usually hung in the homes of believers: It typically occupies a hook on the kitchen wall between the "You Had Me at Woof" plaque and the dog-tongue paper-towel dispenser. The kitchen, as is well known, is the spiritual heart of every human home. By putting the leash on prominent display there, humans offer themselves a daily reminder that they can yoke themselves to the spirit of Dog whenever they choose to link leash to collar.

The leash symbolizes nothing less than the sacred, timeless, eternal union of Man and Dog.

Well, that and, of course, the whole late-night pooping thing.

THE BOOK OF COLLARS

Man's Humanization of Dog

Dog said unto God, *"Say, God, there's something I've noticed after spending some time among humans. Whenever I see their pictures of you, you're always wearing these long robes and have this big white beard. In fact, you look just like a guy—only slightly more annoyed."*

"Ah, yes," said God, *"the whole 'robe and beard' thing. I was wondering when you'd bring that up. . . ."*

"I mean, I never see you wearing robes up here in heaven. In fact, I never see you wearing anything at all."

"I know, I know," said God. *"Man came up with the whole robe idea and pretty much ran with it. Man, you see, loves to make the beings he worships look exactly like him. Crowns and scepters . . . I've never used a scepter in my life! But—and I hate to tell you this— that's nothing compared to what you're going to have to put up with."*

"What do you mean?" asked Dog, trembling ever so slightly.

"You won't believe the stuff they're going to put on you . . ."

I. Outward Signs of Belief

Humans are fond of advertising their attitudes and beliefs with signs and symbols. Just a casual glance at the collection of stickers on a passing car often reveals more personal information than an FBI dossier:

* Christian Republican golfer on board!
* Volvo-driving Democrat with an Ivy League pedigree
* Buddhist shaman vegan Reiki healer who shops at Whole Foods and gets her inner tune-ups at the Chakra Shack
* Atheist Libertarian doomsday prepper at the wheel!
* Bigfoot-hunting, UFO-chasing, Cubs fan (the fantasy hat trick)
* I'm Goth. . . . Fuck off!

Man wants to be known for his beliefs and values. That's because Man *identifies* with his beliefs. "Our beliefs are who we are, man!" Humans strive to let the world know where they stand on everything from religion to politics to music to which celebrity has the best pecs, legs, face, car, and arrest record. By sharing their beliefs, hobbies, and loyalties on bumper stickers, T-shirts, screen savers, and postings on social media, and by demonstrating their tastes and preferences through the products they buy and the places they visit, humans are advertising *themselves*. They want everyone to know, "We've *found it*, by golly! So honk if you love Elvis the way we do, Buy American, Go Green, and, by the way, our kid made the honor role at St. Ignatius Preschool."

Do dogs do any of this stuff? No. They are too mature, and they're having too much fun laughing behind their paws at Man for doing it—and for providing Dog with the greatest show on Earth.

II. Signs of Dogtology

Generally speaking, the more outward signs of a belief a human displays, the more seriously that person takes that belief. For instance, a casual Red Sox fan (assuming such a theoretical being even exists) might sport a "B" hat and a "Yankees Suck" bumper sticker. However, a *die-hard* Red Sox fan will have a "B" logo laser-burned onto his scalp, an inflated Red Sox condom flying from his car antenna, Red Sox underwear worn *outside* of his pants, layers of overlapping Red

Sox tattoos dating back to age six, an army of Red Sox bobblehead dolls in his bedroom that seem to move around on their own at night, and a one-song playlist on his iPod featuring the Dropkick Murphys.

Likewise, you can easily identify Dogtologists by the sheer quantity of dog-themed artifacts that surround them. A Dogtologist, by definition, is more than a casual canine enthusiast. Often she has embraced Dogtology without being consciously aware that she is even practicing a formal belief system. If you were to ask this person what her core beliefs and values were, she might respond, "I'm Jewish and I'm a Democrat. I support the arts and I'm a strong environmentalist." But enter her *home*, and here's what you would see:

- a "Wipe Your Paws" floor mat
- an "I'm the Captain; Get Over It" dog-food dish
- a swarm of dog-themed refrigerator magnets consuming the fridge like flesh-eating bacteria
- a toilet-shaped water dish on the kitchen floor
- a wall clock with paws instead of numerals
- a laptop on the counter logged on to WoofReport.com
- a coffee mug featuring a dog saying, "You want to cut off my WHAT?!"
- a sofa-replica doggie bed with a bone-shaped pillow

The sheer number of dog-themed objects—or *paw-aphernalia*—they surround themselves with is a pretty accurate measure of Dogtologists' faith, whether they realize it or not. In fact, believers demonstrate their faith in two essential ways:

1 By "canine-izing" (i.e., doggifying) the world of humans
2 By humanizing the world of dogs

In both ways, Dogtologists seek to bring the world of the human and the world of the canine closer together. *Really* close together.

III. The Collar

The canine-ization/humanization process between Man and Dog begins with the dog collar. The collar is the way humans all over the world put their human stamp on dogs. A dog with a collar means a dog paired with a human. To a human, nothing says "Dog" more eloquently than a collar. Draw a simple sketch of an empty collar with a few studs on it, and the human mind practically *creates* a dog to fill it in.

The collar has existed since the earliest days of humans and dogs. The collar is the essential piece of gear that every dog allows its human to place upon it. A dog doesn't need to be "broken" before it will wear a collar (such as a horse needs to be before it will accept a bridle). Instead, the dog bows its head and willingly receives the studded leather ring, as if voluntarily taking on humanity's seal of approval. In fact, "ring" might be a better word for it. A collar is much like an oversize wedding ring. When a human places a collar on a dog, the dog, in effect, says to the human, "I pledge my eternal troth to thee," to which the human responds, "Till death do us part."

IV. Love in the Time of Collars

Humans choose their dog collars much the same way they choose their cars: not for the qualities they desire in the product, but for the statement it makes about *them*. Do they want to be perceived, for example, as . . .

- ❧ a successful, mature, golfer type (Lincoln Town Car)
- ❧ a responsible environmentalist (Toyota Prius)
- ❧ a quirky geek (Nissan Cube)
- ❧ a sexy and adventurous entrepreneur, but *not* a totally self-involved, energy-wasting dickhead (Porsche Panamera Hybrid)
- ❧ a soccer mom who secretly hopes to be rescued from suburbia by a bad-boy in a (non-hybrid) Porsche (Honda Odyssey)

- a wealthy survivalist/warrior/post-apocalyptic tribal chieftain (Range Rover)

- a rugged outdoorsman (Jeep Wrangler)

- a not-so-rugged outdoorsman (Subaru Outback)

- a tenured professor at an ivy-covered northeastern college (1974 Volvo)

A dockworker wouldn't drive a pink VW Beetle, an artist in Soho wouldn't drive a Buick Regal, and no one would drive a Pontiac Aztek (and, in fact, no one did).

Humans choose dog collars in much the same way—not so much for what the collar says about the dog, but for what it says about the *human*. The collar is the primary way humans impart their personalities on their dogs. Whether it's the plain, unadorned chain; the pink, buttery-leather "necklace" spelling "PRINCESS" in sequins; the free-spirited bandanna; the weathered brown leather strap with the Harley-Davidson insignia; or the McNative American dream catcher with feathers and healing crystals; the collar is an advertisement for its owner.

Dogtologists can be obsessed with projecting human traits (tastes, values, personalities, even private, unvoiced thoughts) onto their dogs. This fits into an overall pattern: After all, humans have a long history of projecting themselves onto forces of nature and beings they see as greater than them. They give hurricanes names like Bob, they depict Nature as a mother, and they label the ocean angry, the weather fickle, and the sun happy. So it shouldn't be too surprising that Dogtologists opt to humanize dogs. It's the way humans typically handle things of a superior nature. Dogs become walking billboards for our own beliefs.

v. Dogs Doing Random Human Things

What *is* surprising, though, is the endless extremes to which humans portray dogs as people. Take, for example, Man's eternal fascination

with dogs doing random, pointless human things. If you wish to make a human laugh, anytime, anywhere, show him a picture or a video of a dog doing a human activity—any activity. Want to make that same human laugh 3,862 times? Show him 3,862 videos of a dog doing a human activity (even DUDs can be caught laughing at these). A human never says, "If I see another dog driving a boat, I'm gonna scream!" Squirrels or donkeys driving boats? *Meh*. Dogs driving boats? *Hilarious!*

Dogs doing random, pointless human things should not be as funny as it is. But it just *is*. Virtually any human activity can be rendered hilarious by the insertion of dogs in the place of humans. There are no exceptions to this rule. Here are some of the more popular examples:

Dogs driving cars. Place a dog at the steering wheel of any automobile, and presto—instant humor classic! No human has ever *not* laughed at the sight of a dog driving a vehicle. Add a pair of sunglasses to that dog and it's an instant sidesplitting classic. No Dogtologist has failed to put her pup behind the wheel of her car at least once.

Dogs playing sports. YouTube would never have survived for more than a month were it not for its staple product: dogs on skateboards. Of the over four billion videos viewed daily on YouTube, it is conservatively estimated that 3.97 billion of these are videos of dogs on skateboards. Any game or sport can be woven into comic gold by showing a dog as the contestant: A dog shooting pool! A dog with a Wiffle bat in its teeth! And of course, the granddaddy of them all, the *Dogs Playing Poker* series, which has been reproduced more than *The Last Supper* and that Che Guevara photograph combined.

Dogs wearing human clothes. Dogs wearing eyeglasses. Dogs wearing tutus. Dogs wearing the uniform of a doctor, a police officer, a nun, or a farmer. Dogs wearing pajamas, backpacks, evening dresses. Dogs wearing wigs. Dogs wearing sports jerseys. All of these are funny for no good reason. Never *not* funny.

Dogs dancing. Dogs standing on their hind legs and "dancing" is the single most universally chortled-at phenomenon in all of human history, with the exception of the bad guy slipping on a banana peel. Dogs dancing in conga lines = humor squared.

Dogs working at the office. Place a dog in any office-related activity—sitting at a desk, using a computer, making copies, pointing to a pie chart—and you will bring the house down faster than Godzilla playing hopscotch.

Dogs doing everyday activities. Dogs reading, playing instruments, drinking at a bar, smoking pipes, pushing shopping carts, doing laundry, watching the television, playing Xbox, and so on. Who needs Comedy Central?

FOURTH COMMAND

EVERY TIME THOU DOWNLOADETH A HILARIOUS YOUTUBE VIDEO OF A DOG PERFORMING ANY HUMAN ACT, THOU SHALT IMMEDIATELY POST IT ON THE INTERNET AND FORWARD IT TO EVERYONE ON THY CONTACTS LIST.

Dogs talking. And, of course, there's the king of all canine humor: the talking dog. Whether it's a photograph of a dog with human speech bubbles added, an animation of a talking dog, or footage of a real dog with a human's voice dubbed in, a talking dog is surer to get a laugh than a bacon double cheeseburger is to stop a heart.

Switch out dogs for humans in all these scenarios and you have nada. Furthermore, dogs don't seem to find humans doing dog stuff funny. Yet, film a dog at a diner counter drinking coffee, and you've got the next "Gangnam Style" or "Numa Numa" sensation. Show humans a dog with its head on a human pillow or a dog "praying" and you instantly melt every human heart within a twenty-mile radius.

VI. The Humanization of Dogs

Dogtologists don't merely enjoy *images* of dogs doing human things; they actually convince themselves that dogs *are* human. That is, they believe dogs want and need many of the same things humans do. This is one of the great blind spots of Dogtologists. Man's devotion to Dog prompts a desire to "serve" Dog by providing for his every need, yet most humans are woefully incapable of seeing that dogs have their own expressly canine needs and desires. And so Man creates entire multibillion-dollar industries devoted to serving dogs' *imagined* needs.

Grooming and Clipping

Despite dogs doing everything in their power to convince humans that they do not enjoy going to the groomer's, being "Silkwood showered," and having their warm, protective coat shaved and clipped into shapes that would embarrass the bushes at Dollywood, humans insist on knowing better. Humans tell themselves that dogs like to look and smell "pretty." When the dog returns from the groomer's with its few remaining patches of fur knotted into sailor's hitches with pink ribbons, humans say, "Don't you feel better now?" And they interpret whatever response the dog offers as a "Yes, absolutely, and thank you for doing this to me!"—even if the dog runs into her doghouse in the backyard or hides under her favorite blanket and refuses to emerge for hours.

Boarding

Only a couple of generations ago, dog "boarding" was a very simple matter. The dog was chained up in the barn or garage with a week's supply of food and water, a folded-up car blanket, a squeak toy for playing the blues, and a half acre of spread-out newspaper, and told to "be good" while the humans headed off for the Grand Canyon. Admittedly, this was not ideal for the dog, and so boarding kennels came into fashion. As humans continue to humanize dogs more and more, even kennels are being rejected. Today's Dogtologist believes that dogs have the same lodging requirements as white-collar business travelers. Hence, today's upscale doggie inns, doggie hotels, and doggie B&Bs (bed & bark-fest, presumably). In fact, at Dollywood there is a section called Doggywood, which is a temporary boarding facility for tourists' pups. Some of these four-star facilities have such amenities as flat-screen TVs, human-style beds, piped-in music, indoor toilet facilities, and doggie ice cream treats at bedtime. Perhaps for an extra charge, guests can also rent Private Collection videos such as *Duchess Does Dallas* or *Behind the Green Doggy Door*.

Daycare

Hardcore Dogtologists no longer like to leave their dogs alone even for a few hours, so now there are thriving "doggie daycare" centers. Due to the rising cost of doggie daycare, many parents are now being forced to make the agonizing decision to leave their human toddlers alone in the garage all day (with plenty of newspaper, of course) so that their dog may spend the day at The Crate Escape or Canine to Five.

Medical Care

Dogtologists also believe that dogs require a level of medical care that mirrors their own. So they have created a veterinary system that includes waiting rooms, clipboards, stethoscopes, scales, meds, and doggie lollipops for good patients. Dogs are referred to by their names and surnames ("Bowser O'Reilly, please follow me"). In reality, dogs probably require little medical attention; after all, wolves seem to get by fine without semiannual cholesterol checks. Although certain procedures such as vaccinations are important, the trip to the vet is primarily a ritual for the *humans*—to protect themselves from losing their precious pets. There is, of course, one major way in which the canine health-care system differs from the human one: Veterinarians actually spend *time* with their patients and talk to them (an amazing concept, no?).

Clothing and Accessories

Man and Dog are fundamentally different in at least one major way: Dog has built-in clothing, Man does not. One would think this difference would be fairly obvious to all parties concerned, but many Dogtologists feel compelled to purchase their dogs fetching wardrobes of

humanlike clothes. While it may seem obvious that dogs don't actually *need* to wear the Superman costume, ballerina tutu, or rapper bling that humans often dress them in, it is less obvious when it comes to winter jackets, rain slickers, and booties. Many Dogtologists actually believe dogs need these items to brave the great outdoors.

Special Events

Humans also convince themselves that dogs need to mark special events the same way humans do. This not only includes dog birthday parties and stacks of dog presents under the Christmas tree, but can also involve paid professional services, such as the doggie funeral, the doggie obedience-school graduation, and the bark mitzvah. The latter is an increasingly popular coming-of-age party that some Jewish dog owners are hosting for their pups (seriously). In an era where human bar mitzvahs can cost upwards of $50,000, the bark mitzvah is a handy way of exterminating any pesky traces of credit remaining on one's Visa card.

Why do Dogtologists do all of these things? Well, they tell themselves it's to make dogs happier, and that's what they *really believe*. But when was the last time anyone checked in with the dog?

The issue comes down to this: When a Dogtologist looks into a dog's eyes, he sees another *person* looking back and so he can't imagine that his dog would want anything different from what he wants. And, of course, as a practicing Dogtologist, he is determined to *fulfill* all those delicious doggie desires. Dogs put up with all of this nonsense with patience and tolerance perhaps because they appreciate humans' intentions (if not their actual behavior).

VII. Dog Products

By far the most common way humans "canine-ize" their own world and humanize the world of dogs is through the almost infinite variety of dog products they purchase. The main purpose of these products is to cram dogs into a human mold—not an easy task when one species is a six-foot-tall, mostly hairless, bipedal primate driven by materialism, and the other is a furry two-foot-tall canine driven by love (okay, and food).

Canine products include thousands of types of doggie lotions, doggie furniture, dog homes (such as one model that reportedly costs $400,000 and features two bedrooms and a day lounge, a heated spa, a 52-inch plasma TV, self-cleaning dog dishes, and a retinal-scan security system), doggie accessories (including jeweled collars, bone-shaped pendants, and doggie backpacks), and dog toys that replicate human possessions. If one were to add up the price tags of all the doggie stuff in the average Dogtologist's home, it would be enough to put a down payment on a Gulf-stream G650.

While we could fill entire books with examples of these products, here are a few of the more creative options available today:

Dog Christmas antlers. Because nothing tickles a dog's fancy more than masquerading as a wild ungulate.

Doggie high seat (for sitting a dog at a human table). Because, hey, let's take away the one and only aspect of dining with humans that dogs actually enjoy: trolling the floor for scraps.

"Bad Dog" bags of coal. Because not only are dogs ardent students of Yuletide mythology, but they also love receiving "concept" gifts that can't be eaten, played with, or chewed.

Dog Twitter device ("translates" barks into pre-scripted tweets that actually—no joke—get posted on Twitter). Because today's socially aware dog must be concerned with constantly raising his online networking profile.

Dog-collar digital camera. Because what dog doesn't want to amass a huge photo collection of the backs of human knees?

Cell phone–shaped dog pillow. Because dogs require pillows to sleep and because clearly the most logical shape for a dog pillow is an oversize human telephone.

Doggie baby stroller. Because, hey, why not go ahead and take Dog's one opportunity per day to get ten minutes of desperately needed exercise and turn it into yet another passive activity for the convenience and amusement of Man?

Nail "pawlish." Because no eligible beagle bachelorette would leave home without her claws painted Pepto-Bismol pink.

Dog perfume. Because every dog knows nature got it wrong by not making her smell like a strawberry Pop-Tart.

"I Love Bitches" gangsta pendants. Because not only can dogs read, but they also famously love having their necks weighed down by pendulous objects on chains.

These products bring no value whatsoever to the dog. In some cases, however, Dogtologists *do* buy products that genuinely attempt to entertain or help dogs. Of course, these attempts miss the mark just as badly, but at least the human has his heart is in the right place:

Doggie freezer treats. Because what dog wouldn't rather eat frozen sugar water on a stick than a handful of hamburger?

Human crackers. Because nothing says "tasty" to a dog like crackers shaped like tiny, cartoonlike representations of Homo sapiens.

Bone-shaped dog-food dish. Because the moment a dog lays eyes on a bright yellow, concave piece of molded plastic that's straight in the middle with a bulbous, ass-like protuberance on either end, filled with BigValu dog food, the first thing he thinks, "Oh boy, I'm glad I'm eating this great big juicy BONE and not some crap-ass bowl of kibble."

Ball that makes electronic cat noises. Because living with humans doesn't make dogs neurotic enough, they actually require a plastic toy that constantly emits the sound of their natural enemy.

Doggie beer. Because after watching the way humans behave after polishing off a six-pack or two, what dog wouldn't want to join in the festivities?

Edible homework pad. Because dogs adore the whole "dog ate my homework" story.

Stick-shaped toy. Because—wait, are real wooden sticks *really* in that short supply around town?

"Humpable" stuffed toy for male dogs. Because when your dog's sexual frustration reduces him to the point of humping Elmo in the middle of the kitchen floor, what he's probably thinking is, *Gosh, if only this stuffed toy were a tad more anatomically correct.*

That's only a tiny sampling of the literally thousands of products Dogtologists amass for their unsuspecting hounds. There are also gourmet take-out kitchens for dogs, doggie bakeries ("barkeries"), doggie gyms, doggie health spas, and dog chiropractors and masseuses. The only reason there are no sit-down restaurants exclusively for dogs is that no one has been able to figure out how to get dogs to stop tipping 300 percent on their humans' credit cards.

VIII. Dog-Made Products for Humans

So, what's the flipside? Let's take the dog's *pawspective* for a moment. If dogs were able to create products for humans, would they be as insensitive to humans' *real* needs and preferences as humans are to theirs? If so, there might be products under Man's Christmas tree like these:

The Barker-Lounger. A hard, flat, unpadded floor mat Man could curl up on to relax and listen to the nonstop recorded sounds of dogs barking. *Ahh.*

Nasal amplifier. A nose-affixed strap-on device that would increase the intensity of all odors by a factor of 3000 percent.

Ear correctors. Wearable dog-ear-shaped cloth flaps that would correct the congenital design flaw human ears possess.

"Pleased to Meat You." A breath spray that would mask offensive human-breath odors with the powerful smell of raw sirloin steak—or day-old road kill.

Grizzle Pop. Chunks of uncooked beef gristle formed into a pleasing lollipop shape (to make it more visually appealing to humans).

The Pitter-Patter. A device that would attach to the human arm, causing it to engage in nonstop dog patting, for up to five hours on a single charge.

Chia Mia! A liquid solution, inspired by the Chia Pet, that humans could apply to their skin to quickly produce full-body fur. (No, not the formulation used on balding men for decades to no avail.)

The Bladder Pisstol. A device inserted through the urethra into the human bladder, allowing the human to distribute urine more uniformly on trees, rocks, and hydrants. The Bladder Pisstol would regulate bladder output, allowing the human to conserve urine and distribute it consistently over the course of a forty-five-minute walk. Up to 250 separate urinations per hour! Comes in royal blue or in pink for female users.

Ahh . . . the possibilities boggle the imagination.

IX. Humanizing Dog Behavior

Man not only humanizes his dogs through the *things* he buys them, but he also has an unending need to humanize dogs' behavior. As Man's desire to make Dog a full-fledged member of his family has increased, so too has his need to coerce dogs to behave more like him. Humans tell themselves this only helps the dogs lead fuller, happier canine lives, but it's really so humans won't become inconvenienced. After all, do humans train dogs to poo in a special place because it's good for the dog? No. They do it because they don't want their houses to smell like the Bronx Zoo three weeks into a zookeepers' strike.

Man expects dogs to learn impossible sets of household rules, such as "No getting on the couch" (except when humans think it's cute). Or "No eating from the table" (except when humans think it's cute). Or "No barking" (except when it's to alert Man to something he might wish to know). Or "No biting" (unless the one being bitten is an intruder or that unwanted neighbor snooping around to collect the cool lawn mower he loaned you three weeks ago). And of course, "No humping anything canine," "No humping anything non-canine," "No eating food items, "No eating nonfood items," "No staying in the house," and "No going outdoors and tracking in dirt!" Dogs could go neurotic trying to follow all of these contradictory human rules—which might make them nearly as neurotic as a human's own offspring.

Training

Humans even turn to professionals to help modify their dogs' behavior. There are many different schools of dog training, and the methods keep changing every few years—not because *dogs* keep changing, but because Man does (or, more precisely, Man's *relationship* with dogs does). This is a side effect of Dogtology becoming more and more established in the world.

Back in the days when humans viewed dogs as little more than work animals, *negative reinforcement* (striking and punishing) was commonly used. When Man began to evolve and view dogs as beloved pets, *positive reinforcement* (treats and praise) came into play. When Man still clung to the belief that he was the alpha dog in the pack, *dominance training* held sway. Now that Man (Dogtological Man, at least) has begun to view a dog as a confidant, partner, and drinking buddy, so-called *relationship-based training* is the new trend. Dogs patiently accept all these changes with an attitude of *Whatever, dude. Let us know when you change your philosophy again. Till then, let's go chase a stick!*

x. The Enter*train*ment Industry: The Dark Side of Dogtology

Dog training also separates the "mainstream" Dogtologist from the extreme Dogtologist. Extremists take pride in shaping their dogs' behaviors in exotic ways, such as teaching them to "sing opera" or ride a unicycle. This is done for the owners' entertainment, of course, although the owners can't admit this to themselves; they claim the dog loves it (kind of in the same way those stage moms do on *Toddlers & Tiaras*).

In some ways "enter*train*ment" is even more degrading than rubbing a dog's nose in poop or banishing it to the doghouse. Perhaps the most extreme example of entertrainment is the kennel-club dog show. These events are carried out with an air of insouciant upper-crust savoir faire. The dogs are clipped and shaved to look like psychotic My Little Ponies, then rated for "breed purity" by judges who are so rigid and humorless they make Nurse Ratched look like a pole dancer.

Imagine if dogs held human shows and used the same kind of language heard at dog shows:

> **ANNOUNCER:** *"Next up in the working group, the middle-aged Irish American cop. This one is named Sean. You'll notice he's got the standard doughy white skin bred into him by generations of avoiding exercise and drinking in bars. His midsection is pleasantly rotund, brought on by years of Catholic sex-oriented shame and low self-esteem. He has the classic small-to-medium penis typical of the Caucasian varieties, and the slight five o'clock shadow so desirable in the working breeds. Temperament-wise, the Irish-American cop is both quick to anger and quick with a joke. His dark humor is matched only by his passion for Guinness Stout and his love of fiddle music. . . ."*

XI. The Ultimate Act of Humanization

Perhaps the most blatant way humans project humanness onto dogs is by choosing dogs that look like them, or by subtly changing their own appearance to look like their dog's. It's no secret that long-faced humans like long-faced dogs. Short-legged humans like short-legged dogs. Pug-nosed humans like pug-nosed dogs. Clothes factor in, too. Women who dress in "cute" clothes are drawn to poodles. Guys who dress sloppily are drawn to shaggy sheep dogs. Slinky, willowy runway models are drawn to silky-haired, long-legged Afghans. And so forth.

What's going on here? Why do humans like to look like their dogs? Is it just that dogs are great looking? Well, sure, that's part of it. Dogs never have bad hair days. They jump in a pond, shake off, and presto: perfect hair, ready for their close-up. Dogs seem perfectly designed to please the human eye. Yet, they seem to have no desire to look like Man. It's hard to imagine a dog fantasizing about looking like a tall, mostly hairless creature with patches of fur in weird places, gaping nostrils, and strange inside-out-looking ears. But humans seem obsessed with choosing dogs that look like themselves. Why?

Maybe humans choose dogs that mirror their looks as a way of bonding with them, sort of the way human friends dress alike. Or maybe it's because humans want other humans to associate them with their dogs (again, to make that greater connection between Man and Dog). Or maybe it's just the most extreme act of vanity imaginable—humans projecting themselves onto the creature they find most attractive in the world and then convincing themselves that the *dog* is lucky to look like *them*.

Or perhaps something even more profound is going on.

XII. Man Makes Dog in His Image and Likeness

Humans have a long history of portraying deities in human form, tirelessly molding their gods into their own image—from the Olympian gods who looked like slightly seedy bathhouse attendants, to the Indian gods who looked like humans who'd ordered whimsical option packages from the body shop, to the big bearded biker dude of Judeo-Christian fame. Scholars believe this is Man's attempt to reduce the various gods to a form he can relate to. To bring God down to earth, as it were.

But perhaps it's the opposite. Perhaps it's Man's attempt to lift himself up, to strive for divinity. Perhaps Man blends his own qualities with those of a more perfect being so that *he* may be brought closer to perfection. Maybe that's what's going on with Man and Dog. Maybe that's why Man ceaselessly tries to humanize the world of dogs and canine-ize the world of humans. To lift himself up. To bring himself closer to doghood.

Ruff ruff.

BOOK OF BARKS

Communication Between Man and Dog

And God said unto Dog, *"There's something we need to talk about: talking."*

"I've been meaning to talk to you about that," replied Dog. *"Man can use words, but I can't. Seems like a pretty major imbalance in our relationship."*

"It might seem that way," said God, *"but I've actually done you a humongous favor. You see, it is Man's ability to talk that will get him into more trouble than any other capacity he possesses."*

"Why's that?" asked Dog, stretching out his forepaws and gazing up at the Almighty.

"Well, you see, because Man can use words, he will insist on turning everything he sees, hears, and thinks into words. Eventually he'll even figure out how to capture these 'words' on paper. Before long he'll fall in love with the words instead of the things themselves."

Dog tried to imagine what it would be like to love the words "badger pee" more than the taste and smell of the real deal. He couldn't.

"Take me, for example," said God. *"Man will come up with many different words for me, and will also put words in my mouth that I never said. (Good Me, I don't even speak in words!) Then he will literally go to*

war over whose word for me is the right one and which words of 'mine' are truer! Meanwhile, he'll forget about the real me almost completely."

Dog whimpered, "How sad."

"I don't want you to get stuck in the same trap," said God. "By keeping you out of this 'talking' business, I am allowing you to continue to experience your world purely and directly. Your voice will be very limited, and you will use it only when Man allows. What might seem like a handicap is actually a huge blessing. Your verbal silence will allow you to remain light-years ahead of Man, spiritually speaking. But here's the thing—"

"There's always a 'thing' with you," snuffled Dog.

"Man loves the sound of his own voice and will especially enjoy talking to you."

"Why?"

"Because you don't talk back. He does the same thing with me! Man will also put human words in your mouth that you're not really thinking, all for his own amusement. Take it from me: Man will write books and make movies full of stuff I supposedly said, and most of it will be purely his own projections. It will be incredibly annoying."

"Sounds it," said Dog.

"But here's something important to remember. Man only puts words in my mouth because he wants to be closer to me. Imagining me talking to him in his own language is the only way he knows how to . . . connect with me. The same is true with you. Man will imagine you talking to him in human words because he wants to be close to you. In fact, the more Man puts words in your mouth, the more you know he loves you. It's still annoying as crap, but remember, it's done out of love . . . mostly."

I wish I found that reassuring, thought Dog.

"Of course, the real reason he'll bare his soul to you," said God, "is that you're such a good listener. It's a curse you and I share. Believe me, Man will test your listening skills to the utter limit."

"Happy to do my part," said Dog.

"Don't be too quick to say that," warned God.

I. Believe in the Bark

Dogtologists are obsessed with talking to Dog. They talk to their dogs from morning till night, and then again in their dreams. The more extreme the Dogtologist, the more energy he invests in communicating with dogs. But, of course, "communicating" is a bit of a misnomer here, because it implies a mutual exchange of information between two parties. And mutual exchange does not typically occur when Man is one of the parties.

Though barking is usually associated with dogs, it is Man, in fact, who does most of the "barking" in the Man/Dog relationship. Man talks *at* Dog, while Dog patiently sits there looking at Man as if he just phoned a hair salon and ordered an anvil pizza with blue hubcaps—eager to help, but no clue as to what Man is yapping about, or why. And of course, Man is almost totally clueless about what Dog wishes to communicate to *him*. Why? Because Man is so obsessed with talking *to* Dog and *for* Dog that he doesn't pay much attention to the sounds and signals coming *from* Dog. Oy!

Man insists on believing that his own words can be fully comprehended by dogs, and he constantly "translates" the dog's sounds and actions into words he imagines the dog is "trying to say." Double oy!

Human-canine communication takes five major forms. Humans talk:

1 *To* Dog
2 *For* Dog
3 *About* Dog
4 *Through* Dog
5 *Over* Dog

II. Man Talks *to* Dog

Dogs provide an essential communication outlet for humans. Humans *need* to talk to dogs. Perhaps that is because the mere presence of Dog excites the tongue of Man as the Muses inspired the poets of old. Or perhaps it's just because Man couldn't keep his mouth shut even if he used a staple gun, Krazy Glue, *and* duct tape.

Man talks to Dog for many reasons. Three of these are the most common:

1 To create a feeling of *bonding*
2 To issue *"commands"*
3 To talk to Dog in a sacred, *confessional* sense

Bonding Talk (Praise Dog!)

Much of Man's talking to Dog is purely for bonding purposes. Man is insecure about Dog's love for him, so he constantly chatters at Dog in order to feel connected to him. This talk usually occurs in an extremely high-pitched, babyish, singsong tone of voice that humans would never use with adult humans. This voice has the nervous, placating, walking-on-eggshells quality a cartoon butler might use when trying to butter up a spoiled four-year-old master with anger-management issues. ("Does Sugarbooboo want a treat? Of course she does! Of course she does!")

FIFTH COMMAND

WHENEVER TALKING TO DOG, THOU SHALT SPEAK IN THE QUADRUPLE OCTAVE ESCALATION (QOE), THE SAME HIGH-PITCHED STYLE OF BABY TALK THOU MIGHT USE TO TALK A TODDLER OFF A LEDGE.

This eccentric pitch and vocal style is known as the *quadruple octave escalation*, or QOE. Humans probably use this lilting, high-pitched voice because it softens them toward the object of their affection. This also explains why humans use a similar tone with babies (at least until the day they learn to say, "Why does Mommy keep huffing helium?"). When used with dogs, though, the QOE may come across as weirdly submissive (which is odd, considering Man views himself as the master species).

Man seems to believe that just because dogs *can* hear higher-pitched sounds than humans can, they *can't* hear anything lower than a dog whistle. So humans continually address dogs in the QOE—narrating the mundane actions of their lives, asking Dog how his day is going, and trying to explain to dogs, in complex paragraphs, the rationale for requesting that they not pee on the imported loafers or dine from the litter box.

And, of course, above all else, Man uses the QOE to *praise* Dog. This praise is offered, at minimum, on a quarterly-hour basis (or pretty much any time the dog is not actively stealing meat from the counter or dry-humping the landlord's leg). Doggie praise is a truly remarkable phenomenon. In fact, the average Dogtologist cannot go more than three minutes without reminding his dog how good she is. "Good" is the universal unit of dog praise, though it can be embedded in an infinite number of phrasings, such as "Who's a good boy?"; "I see a good doggie over there"; and "You're such a good girl. I want to wear you like a fanny pack."

Bonding talk accomplishes its goal for the human (to make the human feel closer to the pup), but for the dog, not so much. A dog probably recognizes the nonstop QOE barrage as being directed at him. He probably also recognizes, from the hopeful face of the human, that a response of some kind is expected from him. But, since every communication is sung to him in the exact same psycho-kindergarten-teacher tune, the dog has no idea what the human is asking. So the dog offers a noncommittal tail wag, flops on the floor, and lapses into the state of mild anxiety that is the default condition for all dogs living with Man.

Commanding Talk

Humans do nothing to relieve Dog's anxiety by the way they issue commands. (The word "command" here does not refer to the Ten Commands, but to normal, everyday orders.)

Commands are an essential part of human-dog relations, because on rare occasion the human requires the dog to actually *do* something. Commands, however, are a common source of communication breakdown. That's because many Dogtologists are uncomfortable issuing orders, as they feel this is a disrespectful way to treat the being they revere so much. So they frame their commands to Dog as polite requests, couched in terms like "please," "excuse me," and "would you mind?" Dogs, once again, are confused by this. Since the human does not seem to fully grasp exactly what he wants, neither does the dog. And the dog ends up feeling anxious, gnawing on its foot, and suddenly realizing there is a tail connected to its butt, which must be caught.

Some dog-training experts claim that, since dogs are pack animals, they only respond to the alpha dog of the pack. These experts promote a kind of tough love, whereby the human asserts his top-dog status by giving firm commands to the dog. Firm commands do work, but probably for a simpler reason than one might think: clarity. Dogs just want to know exactly what the hell humans *want* already. It's not about who is alpha; it's about *What in the name of God are you asking me to doooo?*

Humans don't realize how wishy-washy and noncommittal they sound to dogs. Dogs tune in to key words like "walk," "ride," or "treat," and to specific intentions, movements, and attitudes. When the human fails to utter key words—or mutters them in a casual, passive way, buried in an avalanche of filler words or meaningless movements—the dog is as lost as a reality-TV star at a theoretical-physics convention. Dog behaviorists confirm this. They have observed that issuing commands to dogs in the following format is remarkably effective:

1   Human states dog's name. This gets the dog's attention and informs it that the human is talking to *it*, not to the television (with which the human also converses on a regular basis).

2   Human then issues a simple, *one-word* command, such as "Come" or "Drop" or "Car," in a firm tone. This is not a negotiation. The human does not frame his command as a polite request, surrounded with words like "if you agree that it might be a good idea." The human does not end his command on a questioning note, like a Valley Girl describing her recent trip to the mall? The human does not wear an expression of desperate hope on his face, as if he'd be more surprised to see his dog obey him than he would to see the president standing behind a McDonald's counter asking him, "Do you want fries with that?"

However, dog behaviorists have noted that issuing commands in the following format, while much more common among Dogtologists, is markedly *less* effective: "Today's the day you get your annual rabies shot, and you know how important that is. I know Pookie hates needles, but Pookie doesn't want to get sick, right? So Mommy has to take you to the vet. If you're good, Mommy will get you a treat on the way home. So what do you say? Ready to go see nice Dr. Carpenter? He might have a treat for you, too! Okay?" Humans cannot help themselves, as they are weakened by the cuteness.

Of course all Pookie hears is "Pookie . . . Pookie . . . treat."

Confessional Talk

Though most dog talk is of the singsong, QOE variety, sometimes Man needs to really *talk* to Dog, bare his soul, *get deep*. Between the neglectful spouse, the nagging boss, and the bickering kids, the dog is often the only "person" in a human's life to whom they can turn for solace.

There is a safety and comfort in talking to Dog that all believers know. In fact, the more serious the Dogtologist, the more she treats the dog as a true confidant, almost as a priest-confessor, sharing with it her darkest secrets, knowing she will not be judged. Or challenged. Or talked back to. Or laughed at.

Unlike human companions, dogs never feel compelled to . . .

* interrupt you to say, "You think *that's* bad, my cousin from Dubuque had it even worse"

* keep signaling "hang on a sec" while checking their text messages

* glance repeatedly at the clock and start edging toward the door

* look at you as if you were a piece of fermented owl poop because you confessed to something you weren't proud of

* say, "I'll tell you what you need to do," and start solving your problem before you even explained what your problem was

* say, "That wasn't very smart, was it?" when it was fairly clear that if you thought your decision was smart, you wouldn't be anguishing over it right now

* focus on the trivial details of your story—e.g., "No, it couldn't have happened on a Tuesday because the garbage men come on Tuesday"—while completely missing your main point

* insert vacant-sounding "ah"s, "uh-huh"s, and "that must have been awful"s into your story while stealing glances at the game on TV

* offer words of "wisdom" like "There's always more fish in the sea" or "Some day you'll look back on this and laugh"

Dog never responds like this to Man. In fact, no matter what a human says in confidence, a dog will listen intently, and when Man is done, the dog will look at him with an expression that says, "I love you. Let's go eat something, then chase a ball!"

Dogs are simply better listeners than humans. Period. Even though they don't understand all of Man's words, they seem to grasp the emotions and intentions behind them. They seem to know when their humans are hurting and are able to empathize and give them space. And Dog always has the perfect solution to life's troubles: Go eat and then rip the stuffing out of a toy!

III. Man Talks *for* Dog

Talking *to* Dog is only part of Man's daily output of canine verbiage. Man also talks *for* Dog, night and day. Man feels an endless need to put human words in Dog's mouth.

Every Dogtologist creates a special "voice" for their dog and carries on "two-way" conversations with their pet that would make a Vegas ventriloquist jealous. The default voice humans use to speak for dogs is often a slightly dopey high-pitched drawl that is weirdly at odds with the insightful comments they put in dogs' mouths. Some humans even choose character-actor-type voices for their dogs. These voices, of course, are based on human stereotypes. No one gives a poodle a Sylvester Stallone–like voice ("C'mon, Frufie, les go for a walk . . . Eyyy, wassamatta witchu?"), or a bulldog the voice of a Hollywood hairstylist ("Oh, your face is so delicious I wanna smear ice cream on it 'n lick it off; you're so cuuute!"). No. Never happens. However, whatever voice the human chooses for the dog becomes its voice for life.

So, how do dogs feel when humans talk for them? That's hard to say, but humans can probably remember how *they* felt as kids when their parents spoke for them without asking for any input. "Oh, Susie *loves* spending her weekends with Smelly Sally—that's her favorite auntie!"

Humans love imagining dogs talking in human tongues but have very little tolerance for hearing the actual voice of Dog. In fact, they enjoy the barks and whines of dogs about as much as they enjoy the sound of a Chinese gong at two in the morning. Humans prefer dogs to remain silent and to "speak" only in the imagined language of humans. But that fantasy occurs only in Chet and Bernie mysteries.

Talking Dogs in Art and Literature

Humans speak not just for their own dogs, but also for dogkind in general, as a way to entertain themselves. Talking dogs are one of mankind's most popular forms of amusement, appearing frequently in fairy tales, children's stories, comics, books, animated cartoons, ads, and movies.

Some of the earliest known talking-dog stories were Aesop's fables such as "The Mischievous Dog" and "The Dog and the Hare." In these stories, the dog was often seen as conniving, stupid, greedy, and lowdown—the buffoon that taught other characters lessons by virtue of his goof-ups. It wasn't until the twentieth century, with the growing Dogtology movement, that talking dogs began to take on other personas.

One of the earliest animated talking dogs was Bimbo in the Betty Boop cartoons. Bimbo said things like "Ooh, baby" and "I like that" as he stared at Betty while she gyrated her booty—talk about giving a dog a bone!

After Bimbo came one of the oddest dog duos in history, Goofy and Pluto. They were likable but dumb. Goofy walked on two legs, wore clothes, lived in a human house, and spoke gems like "Gawrsh, Pluto, let's go find Mickey, hyuck, hyuck" in perfect English. Meanwhile, Pluto wore a dog collar and no clothes, lived in a doghouse, didn't talk, and acted like Goofy's pet. A little kinky if you think about it.

In the later part of the twentieth century, talking dogs began to take on more smarts than their human owners. There was the superhero, Underdog; Ren, the hot-tempered Chihuahua, from *The Ren and Stimpy Show*; Mr. Peabody, the scientist dog with the pet boy named Sherman; Scooby-Doo, the crime-solving dog; and Brian Griffin, the boozy canine intellectual living in a household reeking of dysfunction on *Family Guy*.

Literature is now full of dog protagonists, narrating best-selling novels from the dogs' points of view. There are also dogs making Twitter posts, writing blogs, selling products on TV, and offering advice on how to handle crime. Dog talks, Man listens. Humans are fascinated by hearing dogs' perspective on things. But, of course, it's all still humans talking *for* dogs. After all, what would a dog tweet if it could? "Enough with the Waggin' Train already. Give us some freakin' bacon!" Maybe.

IV. Man Talks *About* Dog

When Dogtologists are deprived of the opportunity to talk *to* and *for* dogs, they fill the aching void by talking *about* dogs. Obviously, dogs are the primary topic of conversation for Dogtologists. Not current events. Not work stuff. Not kids and spouses. Dogs. Dogtologists talk about dogs in the news, dogs on YouTube, dogs in fiction, dogs in the neighborhood. But of course, most of all, they talk about their own dogs. These conversations have two possible themes:

1 My dog is so smart.

2 My dog is so cute.

My dog is *so* smart

Dogtologists are obsessed with sharing evidence of their dogs' intelligence. Every Dogtologist is convinced that *her* pup is president of the Canine Mensa Society. The evidence for this usually boils down to this: The dog did a random thing that accidentally mimicked human speech or behavior. "I said to Bobo, 'Is Santa coming tomorrow?' and he went and sat down by the fireplace. He's a genius! I sure hope he likes what I got for him for Christmas."

On a daily basis, the Internet is flooded with videos of bulldogs "singing" and Jack Russell terriers sweeping floors. Humans can't believe how smart these dogs are! Meanwhile, humans are almost totally oblivious to the way dogs use their *real* intelligence, such as training their humans to give them a treat every time they stop barking.

My dog is *so* cute

Dogtologists are also compelled to carry on lengthy conversations about their dogs' cuteness. Talking about cuteness is about as effective as verbally describing a sight gag from a movie. "You should have seen the way she was sleeping with her nose in my shoe!" The fact that you *didn't* see it is not enough to prevent the Dogtologist from continuing to try to describe what can only be ooh'd and aww'd about when actually *seen*. But Dogtologists always seems to believe that if they offer someone just one more piece of evidence proving their dog's cuteness, everyone will *finally* agree with their master thesis: "My dog is the Number One Cutest Dog in the World!"

v. Man Talks *Through* Dog

One of the most important roles dogs play in the homes of human beings is to provide a vehicle through which the humans can indirectly discuss uncomfortable but important matters that may otherwise be difficult or impossible to discuss (except through $300-per-hour shrinks). In these situations, one might say that Man talks *through* Dog. Dog's role in these highly sensitive matters is to passively serve as the icebreaker, the go-between, the messenger, the psycho-fur-apist.

In human families, communications tend to break down more often than a '76 AMC Pacer with stripped transmission gears and a rebuilt engine. So, humans turn to dogs to help them sort it all out. Humans talk through dogs for many reasons . . .

To Relieve Tension

Sometimes, after spouses have had a falling-out and the tension is so thick a person could stab it with corncob holders and take a bite of it, the only solution is to make a joke in the dog's voice. "Yo, could someone open a window in here? This place is so filled with negative energy it could power the city of Detroit." If the joke works, yay, problem solved. If the joke flops, just blame it on the dog. Win-win for the human.

To Criticize Someone Without Owning It

If, for example, the husband is playing his electric guitar and the wife doesn't want to hear it, she can avoid sounding like a nagging whiner by saying, in the dog's voice, "I wish my dad would stop making that noise." Now it's the *dog* that hates the guitar playing, not the wife! And, if the husband wants to do a quick "back atcha" with the criticism, he can retort (yes, in his variation of the dog's voice), "Hey, my groupies don't seem to mind it all that much." To which the wife can parry as the dog saying, "Oh, really? Those two guys still coming to your little shows?" This fun can go on until the dog simply trots out of the room, shaking his head and feeling confused as to why the humans are talking like a couple of morons again.

To Deliver Messages

When a husband and wife are officially not speaking to one another after a fight, they can relay messages to each other by sharing their plans aloud with the dog while in earshot of one another. For example, the husband might say, "Well, Bowser, I guess I'll go practice my guitar in the garage, won't I? Yes, I will. Yes, I will," and the wife might roll her eyes and stomp out of the room with the dog following behind, shaking his head.

To Resolve Conflict

After a major family blowout, talking through the dog is a great way to make peace. All it takes is for someone to say "Everybody still loves *me*, though, right?" in the dog's voice, and the conflict is on its way to being forgotten. Unless, of course, the other person replies "Blow it out your rear, *Bowser*" in their own voice, in which case it may be time to go ahead and start dividing up the household property and Googling "divorce lawyers."

VI. Man Talks *over* Dog

Most often when vocalizing around Dog, humans do not even make a token attempt at two-way communication. It is simply a case of

Man talking *over* Dog and Dog being forced to put up with it. Not only do we scream over dogs the moment they make the slightest attempt to speak in their native tongue (i.e., growling and barking), but we also fill the air with human sound eighteen hours a day, dominating the aural environment, without any regard as to whether our dog wants to hear it or not. In those rare moments when we're not talking live with our mouths, we're playing *recorded* sounds of human voices from TVs, sound systems, computers, and iPads. We subject dogs to *our* music, *our* movies, and *our* buzzing, screeching machinery, all day long, and they have no mechanism for shutting us up, no choice about whether to listen to *us* or not. Of course, we tell ourselves our dogs are chill with our noises, to assuage our guilt. "My dog *loves* Metallica . . . really."

Many humans do not even give their dogs a break when they leave the house for the day. They play human sounds on the radio to "keep the dog company while I'm gone." What the *dog* is probably thinking as the human reaches for the on button is, *Please God no! How 'bout a few hours of peace and quiet?* Sorry, Milo. Now instead of listening to the sounds of nature with your amazing ears, you get to be subjected to a six-hour *Car Talk* marathon with Click and Clack, the Tappet Brothers, with the volume turned up to 9. Think you can escape by going to the living room? Nope, we've left Animal Planet going on the TV. Why? Because we know how much you love animals. Because, you know, *you're* an animal.

We assault dogs with our sounds continually and yet we get hugely annoyed with them if they yip at the UPS truck for eight entire seconds. Some humans even go to the extreme of using muzzles and shock collars to quiet their dog—not only so the dog "owner" won't be bothered, but so the neighbors won't be bothered either. We can't force muteness on other humans, so we exercise that power on dogs.

Dogs should have a "paws" button they could press that would stop all human sound for up to sixty seconds and allow them to reboot their brains whenever necessary.

When you add up all the various ways Man talks to Dog, you realize that dogs are virtually never free from human speech. This "begs" a fundamental question: Why is Dog at the center of so much of Man's vocal noisemaking?

VII. Swear to Dog ("Prayer" for Dogtologists)

What is it about Dog, a being that remains silent 99 percent of the time, that invites so much nonstop chatter from Man? Well, perhaps the answer is in the question itself. Dog remains silent. By doing so, Dog plays the role of "blank slate," allowing Man to project his thoughts, feelings, and words onto him (not unlike the way Man projects his words and thoughts onto another famously silent being).

Dog is maddeningly nonverbal, so Man feels the need to speak *for* him. But, of course, *many* things in Man's world are nonverbal—goldfish, ashtrays, doorknobs, picture frames, geckos, bowling balls... The list goes on. Why is Dog singled out for so much human speech? The simple answer: because Man is deeply in love with Dog. And so Man projects his words and voice onto Dog, then feels closer to him as a result.

But maybe something even more profound is at work here. Perhaps Man's constant vocalizing with dogs is something akin to... prayer. After all, nearly every form of worship on Earth involves some form of repetitious vocal sound. This might be praying, humming, chanting, singing, reciting mantras, or shouting, "Can I get a *witness*?" (Or, in the case of televangelists, "Can I get your Master-Card number?") Reverence just seems to inspire humans to make sounds. Perhaps that's what the nonstop chatter of the dedicated dog lover is. A form of prayer.

Does this seem farfetched? It shouldn't. When you think about it, what is the primary purpose of prayer? (Besides, of course, trying to weasel out of the consequences of your own actions and lying about the ways you will become a better person if a higher authority saves your ass yet again.)

VIII. The "Voice of Dog"

Science claims Man to be a "higher" species than Dog, often citing as evidence Man's ability to speak by using words. Even if dogs could use words, would they chat insistently like humans? Perhaps not. If blessed with the ability to speak like humans, a dog's vocabulary would still be limited to the important things in life. Here are some things a dog might say:

- "Hi, it's *great* to see you!"
- "Let's play!"
- "I want to be close to you right now."
- "Hey, rolling over means it's time to rub my belly."
- "I need your help with something."
- "You totally rock!"
- "I'm hungry."
- "I'm thirsty."
- "What a great day!"
- "I'm scared."
- "I'm not in the mood for that right now."
- "Go away."
- "*Look out!*"
- "Mailman approaching at two o'clock!"
- "I'm in a goofy mood, how about you?"
- "You shamed me for something I don't understand."
- "I love you, *I love you*, I LOVE YOU!"

Dogs don't have any trouble communicating these ideas *without* words, so why do humans have trouble doing so, even with the blessing of speech? Wouldn't it be great if humans learned how to just say simple, direct things to one another, such as "You're my friend," and "I want you to pay attention to me now," and "When I roll over that means I want you to rub my belly," instead of hiding behind walls of words. If and when that ever happens, then human relationships might actually start to work better than a crosswalk button in downtown Manhattan. Maybe Dog figured this all out a long time ago and, as usual, is patiently waiting for Man to catch on.

IX. Learning to Hear the Voice of Dog

Though dogs seem strangely uninterested in learning to speak a language, they do seem to recognize how important words are to humans, so they make an effort to learn a basic vocabulary. They seem to know how much it pleases Man when they respond to "Get the ball," "Who wants a treat?" or "For the love of God, stop licking that!"

Man, on the other hand, makes little effort to learn how to communicate with dogs on their own level. Dogtologists often claim they would love their dogs to talk to them. Humans often wish, for example, that dogs could tell them what is wrong with them when they are hurt or sick. But the truth is, if humans *could* understand dogs, they'd probably hate it. Humans' egos couldn't handle it if their dogs told them things like, "You know what? I'm not feelin' the love for you today, Ma," or, "That was you singing in the shower just now? I thought a raccoon got caught in the blender." And Man would *really* be crushed to hear, "To be completely honest with you, I'd rather go live with your ex. Better treats, more squeak toys."

Humans aren't really interested in seeing things from the dog's point of view. Yet, if the two-leggeds would take just *one hour* to learn some basic ways dogs interpret the world and how that interpretation affects their communications, it might eliminate 90 percent of the misunderstandings between the two species. For example:

❋ To humans, facing a dog directly and reaching out to pat its head means, "I come in peace." But to dogs it means, "Aggressive primate attempting to manually remove my cranium."

❋ When a dog curls up the corners of its mouth, it is not smiling at the human, but saying, "I am feeling threatened by you and am about to attempt reconstructive surgery on your throat."

❋ Hugging tightly means "I love you" to humans. To dogs, it means, "I am going to crush you, python-style, and then cook you with potatoes and carrots." (Okay, maybe not that—but one never knows, what with the vivid imagination of Dog!)

Those are just a few examples. There's also the huge variety of sounds that dogs make in a futile attempt to communicate with Man. Dogs woof, snarl, rumble, growl, whine, whimper, yelp, squeal, howl, bay, rumph, snuffle, yip, moan, and arf. Each of these sounds has meaning, according to scientists. Unfortunately, Man dismisses all of these as "annoying dog noises." *But,* should a dog make a sound that accidentally resembles a *human* word, *then* we pay rapt attention. Stop the presses! Alert the media! "Spike said, 'Love you'!" Suddenly we're calling everyone on our contacts list and trying to get booked on the late-night talk-show circuit. Spike's video goes viral, gets six million hits on YouTube, and we've got our own reality show on E!.

Meanwhile, Spike is sitting in the corner trying to tell us, in his native voice, that, no, he was actually trying to say that the house next door is on fire. Now he has an inferiority complex because he realizes he's not as brilliantly communicative as the Jetsons' dog, Astro.

x. Listen Like a Dog: Making Your Mark

All Dogtologists, by definition, want to honor dogs, respect them, and treat them with dignity. But that will never happen as long as humans fail to accept the fact that Dog is a barking, yipping, howling being. Only when humans truly accept the voice of Dog in all of its forms will they be able to begin to *listen* to what it's saying. And then perhaps true human and dog communication may begin to occur.

Maybe then dogs will finally be able to explain enduring mysteries, such as why they lap up toilet water like it's Dom Pérignon. And maybe humans will finally be able to explain to dogs things like, "The purpose of the vet's needle is not to elicit a confession, but to make the sickies go away."

Perhaps the true test for how well humans have learned to truly communicate with dogs would be this: Could a human being sit for just ten solid minutes while the dog barks, without slamming their palms over their ears and yelling at the dog to shut up? Well, okay, that may be asking a bit too much of a human, but that's essentially what dogs do for Man, day in and day out. They just listen. (They have no choice; they're being held captive!)

BOOK OF HYDRANTS

Rites and Rituals of Dogtology

I. The Importance of Ritual

Every religion, movement, and belief system has its own unique rituals. In fact, rituals are a big part of what *defines* a religion or belief. Just the fact that many humans hold an idea in their heads is not enough to make it a religion. Otherwise, there would be a Church of My Boss Is a Giant Nimrod, a Church of You Would Drink, Too, If You Had My Life, and a Church of I'm *Too* Nice—That's My Problem. No, it's the *rituals* that make a belief system official.

A ritual is an act that has symbolic meaning. Buddhists and Hindus recite mantras. Jews avoid pork and go to synagogue on Saturday. Wiccans dance naked in the moonlight and drink . . . whatever it is they drink in the night under the moon.

Some rituals are purely symbolic, such as Catholics getting a dash of ash on their foreheads on Ash Wednesday. Others serve both a practical *and* symbolic purpose, such as the Seder dinner (known informally as the Bow and Chow). Dogtology too has its own slate of rituals. In fact, a quick study of the behavior of dedicated believers would reveal that their lives actually revolve completely around Dogtological rituals. Some of these rituals take place daily; others take place weekly, monthly, or at special times on the Dogtology holiday calendar.

II. Dogtological Rituals

There are three basic types of ritual in Dogtology. First are the type that are carried out entirely by humans and that primarily serve the emotional, physical, and mental needs of humans:

Morning Worship. Upon seeing the dog in the morning, before overseeing the Morning Crouch (a ritual performed by dogs), the human lavishes nonstop praise on the pup, in the quadruple octave escalation (QOE), revving the dog into a frenzy, until its bladder is ready to explode.

The Daily Viewing and Forwarding. *After* the Morning Crouch, the Dogtologist rushes to her laptop, tablet, or smartphone to view whatever dog videos have accumulated in her various inboxes overnight, and then forwards them to all of her contacts. This ritual takes priority over childcare, getting to work on time, and household chores (especially among those deep Dogtologists whose dog is their only real "child").

The Symbolic Good Behavior Request. Once per day, often before the Giving of the First Treat, the human symbolically "demands" that the dog perform one act of obedience, such as "Sit" or "Give me your paw" or, if the dog is a border collie, "Please balance my checkbook." The purpose of this ritual is for the human to reassure herself that she is in charge of the household so that she may now surrender control to the CEO (Canine Executive Officer) for the remainder of the day.

The Bedtime Tuck-ins. This is a complex, time-consuming set of nighttime rituals, unique to each Dogtologist, designed to enable the human to emotionally separate from the pup for the next seven or eight hours. It can involve kisses, hugs, treats, praise, songs, stand-up routines, and, in rare cases, incense burning and lying on the floor and letting the dog slobber all over them.

The Buying of the Doggie Birthday, Christmas, Hanukkah, Kwanzaa, Halloween, Easter, Valentine's Day, Egg Salad Day, and

National Dog Day Presents. These are recurring calendar-based rituals in which gift offerings are made to Dog so the human may enjoy the holiday, guilt free.

Another type of ritual is performed *by* dogs and serves the actual needs *of* dogs. Dogtologists are involved in these rituals, too, and must incorporate them into their own ritual behavior. These include:

The Morning Crouch. An outdoor excretory ritual that can turn into an *indoor* excretory ritual if the human fails to get the dog out the door within seventeen seconds after wake-up.

The Barking at / Chasing after / Mauling of the Man in Uniform. An ancient canine ritual, expanded in the modern era to include FedEx, UPS, and cable guys.

The Evening Sofa Shuffle. Every evening the dog will somehow misdirect the human's attention and then magically appear, curled up contentedly on the forbidden sofa.

The Treat Trigger. Every dog custom-designs a unique and "adorable" behavior, tailored specifically for its human(s), which triggers the human to ceremonially offer it treats.

Finally, some rituals have evolved to mutually serve the needs of both the human *and* the dog:

The Sacramental Filling of the Vessels. Before the humans can eat a bite or drink a drop in the morning, the dog is given fresh food and water, firmly cementing the pecking order of the home for both species.

The Rapture. Every time the human and canine reunite after a separation, they renew their bonds with a feverish greeting ritual that can include running like a rocket through the house, jumping up and down, crouching, wriggling, and accidental bladder release (usually, but not always, on the dog's part).

The Walk, or "Walkies" (*see* **Leashes: IX**). The Walk is the daily ritual that brings the human and the canine together in ecstatic spiritual union—and provides the opportunity to leave a fresh gift on the front lawn of the neighbors with the twenty-foot inflatable Santa.

The Purging of the Plates. This is a symbiotic ritual that benefits the human because it facilitates the removal of stubborn traces of egg, melted cheese, and béarnaise sauce from dinner plates before they go into the dishwasher, and benefits the dog because it provides a small sampling of nutriment that doesn't come in a twenty-pound bag.

These are just a few of the countless rituals of Man and Dog. In fact, an examination of the daily behavior of average Dogtologists would show that humans practice more dog-related rituals than rituals related to their other religious faiths, their politics, their jobs, their social causes, their families, or their own self-care combined.

Most human-canine misunderstandings revolve around the two species' mutual inability to grasp and appreciate the other's rituals.

III. The Daily Hydrant Posting

One of the most universal, yet misunderstood, rituals of dogs is the Daily Hydrant Posting, which humans mistake for a simple urinary act. Humans and dogs agree on one thing: All dogs *must* and *will* pee on every hydrant within a four-mile radius. In fact, if a hydrant is not available, the dog will cause one to manifest out of thin air. So, the act of hydrant peeing is a given. But all understanding stops there.

From the human's perspective, the hydrant is nothing but an obligatory stop on the Walk, to be gotten over with as quickly as possible. The human is clueless about the meaning and importance of the hydrant to the dog. Thus, the human "patiently" waits up to eighty-seven seconds while the dog sniffs the fireplug a couple of times and adds a fresh squirt of its own; then he drags the dog off to continue the Walk. The dog, of course, has only just begun its ritual. Sniffing and peeing on the hydrant holds great symbolic meaning for

Dog. The hydrant, in fact, is not a mere pit stop for a dog, but the focal point of the entire Walk.

War of the Hoses

Why is it that, of all the objects dogs could ritually pee on, they have chosen the man-made object known as the fire hydrant to be their favorite? After all, they could have chosen rocks, tree stumps, bushes, cats, potted plants, or slow, elderly gentlemen. And of course they do pee on all of those things, as well as on the occasional wheelchair ("Sorry, humans, our bad." —Sincerely, Dog), but they single out hydrants for special urinary attention. A possible explanation leaps to mind. Think about what a hydrant represents. It is a unit of plumbing used by a very particular type of human—namely, the humans in uniform who ride on the big, loud trucks. Everyone knows that dogs have an issue with every male human wearing a quasi-military uniform, but dogs seem to have a particular issue with firefighters. Why is this? Maybe, just maybe, it has something to do with these irrefutable facts:

* Firefighters drive the vehicles that make the one sound known to totally scramble dogs' brains: the siren!

* Firefighters have big, scary, weird-shaped heads like that Darth Vader guy, whom humans—and by way of loyalty, canines—hate and fear.

* Every time you see a firefighter, a huge fire has broken out (evidence that the job of the firefighter seems to be to burn buildings down).

* Firefighters kidnap Dalmatians and place them on the front of their trucks as hostages.

* Firefighters use *hoses*—one of Dog's worst enemies—and not just simple garden hoses (which are bad enough), but rather the howitzers of the hose world.

* And last but not least: When they're not burning buildings down, firefighters spend their time rescuing cats! *What the #%!#?*

Maybe it's no coincidence that dogs have singled out the one object that is most closely associated with firefighters to urinate on from morning till night: the fireplug. It's a statement.

Not an implausible theory. In fact, it may have legs.

IV. Whizzbook

Whatever the *symbolic* reasons for choosing the hydrant to pee on are, it is clear that the hydrant has developed a highly significant purpose in the canine world. That is, it has become nothing less than a social media portal—a canine version of Facebook, Whizzbook if you will. Dogs post/download on Whizzbook by squatting down or lifting a leg. Dogs read/upload each another's posts by sniffing.

Humans say that a picture is worth a thousand words. For dogs, on the other paw, a dash of pee is worth a *million* words. Dogs can extract more information from sniffing a tiny blast of urine (mixed with emissions from dogs' scent glands) than humans can glean from chatting for hours online. This art of urine-based tweeting was known as "storypeeing" in the pre-Internet era. Sniffing pee can tell a dog . . .

- which local gals are in heat and looking for action
- which dogs come by here every day and which ones have only dropped by to leave a "guest post"
- which dogs have recently hooked up with each other and whether that hookup has led to any awkward conversations in the vet's office
- which dogs have been away on vacation and which holiday hotspots they visited while they were away
- whether any of the local dogs have a touch of the distemper
- what the other dogs have been eating lately and who's been sampling the local wildlife or road kill ("How's the mashed weasel around here?" "Not bad, not bad at all.")

whizzbook

Here we are lying on the beach on Grand Canine Island.

Skipper Jackson Bring me some Rover's Rum from the duty-free shop!

Reggie 19 Dude, love the "duty-free."

This bitch is sooo hot!!!!

Bella Curve No way that tail is real; bet she's had some work done.

Dirty Boxer I'd still chase it! LMAO!

Good eats down at the blind curve on the highway;)

Mohr Bacon The servings are huge, but you always feel rushed.

Trixie M Hope it's grass-fed organic.

Frisbee Fanatic Dang, I'm on the Kibble Cleanse.

In other words, dogs post many of the same, er, "droppings" around their neighborhoods that humans post on sites like Facebook, MySpace, and Twitter. In fact, why humans waste all of their pee in one place when they're outdoors can drive a dog nuts. When the (usually male) human stops and voids his entire bladder on a single tree, the dog looks on in stunned disbelief, thinking, *Duuude! What part of this peeing thing don't you get?! That's valuable stuff— you don't go dumping it all in one place!* Dog, on the other hand, conserves its urine so it can make as many Whizzbook posts in as many spots as possible. To dump all of its pee in one spot would be like us sending 147 tweets on Monday morning, then none for the rest of the week.

Perhaps someday dogs will join the virtual revolution, as humans have, even start an Internet site called eHydrants.com, on which they'll learn to make virtual marks on virtual hydrants, exchanging their personal data online. eHydrants.com could serve as a doggie dating site. Hookups could be prearranged, and studs could meet bitches with whom they felt mutually com*paw*tible. All very sanitary and urine free. Maybe humans could interact with their dogs online, too. Humans would love this, because then they could turn the Walk into a virtual experience, eliminating any reason whatsoever to ever vacate the couch. But for now, dogs insist upon staying frustratingly real.

v. Mud, Dead Fish, and the Ritual of the Bath

It is important for humans to understand canine sniffing rituals, because these activities hold the key to solving so much of our misunderstanding of Dog. It comes down to this: Humans can't even *begin* to appreciate the magnificence of the senses of Dog.

While humans have about six million odor-receptor sites in their nose, dogs have *hundreds* of millions. The entire canine brain is built around smell. This means that you can't keep a secret from a dog. Think no one knows about your hidden stash of Little Debbie banana cakes? Ha! Think no one knows how often you and your special someone engage in, um, you know (this is a *family* book, after all). Think again! Dogs can even tell chronological time based on the fading and deterioration of overlapping smells. Odor-wise, humans live in a stick-figure cartoon; dogs live in *Avatar 3D*.

Because dogs have such extraordinary senses, they take *everything* in with their noses and tongues (in much the way humans do with their eyes). Two-leggeds, by contrast, are very judgmental about smells and tastes. It's either "Ahh, nice!" or "Eww, gross!" So they attempt to surround themselves only with "good" smells. Humans would never consider *tasting* a smear of brown goo on a tree or sticking their face in a Dumpster and inhaling deeply, unless appearing on an episode of *Fear Factor*. Putting a human in charge of the odor-based decisions in a household—and that's what we do—is like hiring a sea cucumber to referee a basketball game.

Dogs' and humans' differences over odors come to a head around the rituals of dog hygiene. As the nasally challenged party, Man constantly bathes Dog to remove "bad" odors. This involves dousing the dog in a chemical shampoo with a "floral" scent that smells about as much like real flowers as that deodorant soap actually smells like springtime in Ireland.

On the other hand, nothing pleases a dog more than to roll in a nice, ropey coil of fox doo. The subtle layers of fragrance in a well-aged braid of vulpine crap tell an intriguing story to the dog and seem to please it as much as the delicate nose of a fine wine pleases a human. But humans are frightened and appalled by such odors. Thus, the ritual of the bath is quickly enacted.

Upon stepping from the bath and being told, "Don't you smell pretty?" the dog immediately heads out to the woods to roll around in dirt, leaves, trash heaps, mysterious-looking excrement piles, and whatever else will help restore the dog to olfactory perfection. This triggers the ritual bath routine all over again, in an endless cycle of wash, un-wash, wash, un-wash, perpetuating the fortunes of both Johnson & Johnson and Petco alike.

VI. "Voiding" Rituals

Just as humans cannot imagine the vast amount of information dogs exchange via their pee and poo, dogs cannot seem to understand the *lack* of attention humans give to their own waste products. The very fact that humans call it "waste" is significant; if dogs used words, they might call it "the good stuff." The way humans waste their waste must seem truly mystifying to dogs. It would be the equivalent of someone writing a long letter to a friend, putting it in a hand-decorated envelope, and then placing the envelope into a paper shredder. To a dog, that's what humans do when they flush away their waste, because it contains their entire life story; it's an essay on their health level, their stress level, the foods they've been eating, the places they've been hanging out, their love life, work life, home life, and the way they've been treating themselves.

VII. The Potty (Pawty) Party

The Potty Party is a ritual that takes place whenever the human goes to the bathroom. The dog dutifully follows the human into the room and lies down near the toilet until the human's deed is complete. If the human tries to keep the dog out, the dog will whine, bark, pace, pant, whimper, or attempt to tunnel under the bathroom door with its forepaws until the human relents and lets it in.

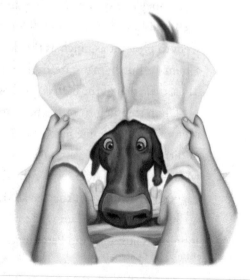

Why are dogs so driven to be in the bathroom with humans? Perhaps they feel a need to at least *try* to prevent us from flushing away our treasures, the same way humans feel a need to prevent Dog from sampling the delicacies of the litter box. Then again, perhaps there are other explanations for the Potty Party:

- Maybe dogs notice the way *humans* watch *them* when they do their duty, and they're just trying to return the favor. Loyalty at its finest.

- Maybe dogs have observed female humans going to the bathroom as a team and are trying to emulate that apparent pack behavior.

- Maybe dogs are simply trying to keep an eye on the toilet lid. They don't understand why some humans insist on closing it, thereby preventing the dog from drinking the most aromatic water in the entire house. (Male humans are much more accommodating to dogs in this regard . . . unless there's a nit-picky female human in the home who keeps after the male about closing the lid, in obviously mean-spirited attempts to keep the toilet water away from said dog.)

- Maybe dogs feel a need to nasally scan the "output" of humans, to make sure they are healthy and happy. After all, a sick human means no Walk.

- Maybe dogs are better at the *People* magazine crossword puzzle than humans suspect, and just want to lend their support.

VIII. The "Other" Potty Party

Then, of course, there's the other kind of Potty Party ritual that every dog owner knows about. That is the need for the dog to occasionally soak our $1,000 Oriental carpet with liquid gold or top it off with a monster helping of double-chocolate soft-serve. Clearly, the dog is trying to make a statement; otherwise, he would deposit his "accident" on the linoleum, where it could be easily cleaned up.

What is the perfectly housebroken dog thinking when he decides, out of the blue, *Today seems like a good day to drop a steaming pile of feces in front of the Blu-ray player*? The answer to that puzzle may never be known, but maybe it's hidden among the following possible thoughts of Dog:

- *There! That's how you do it, for cryin' out loud! You don't flush it down the drain!*

- *You want to know why I did it? Well, I've explained myself quite clearly,*

*right there in my pee and poo. All you have to do is sniff and inter-
pret. . . . Oh, I forgot, you humans have no clue how to do that.*

❧ *I thought the house could use some freshening up. Kind of the way you
freshen up my bed with that olfactory-nerve-destroying gas bomb you
call Febreze.*

❧ *Garbage in, garbage out. How 'bout a change of menu around here?*

❧ *Here's my review of that* Beethoven's Christmas Adventure *movie you
forced me to watch with you last night.*

Or maybe Dog is simply thinking, *Every once in a while I'm
gonna do this kinda thing. Right here on your beloved Persian. Why?
Because I'm a DOG. Deal with it, all right?*

IX. Rituals of the Bedroom

Just as the dog ritually joins the human for the Potty Party, there is an
unwritten rule that dogs are also allowed to join humans for the rituals of the Changing of the Clothes, the Taking of the Shower, and
the Having of the Sex. Neither party, dog nor human, seems quite
sure how or when this rule was first established, nor do they seem
100 percent clear on its significance, but still the rule stands and the
ritual carries forth.

Someone to Watch Over Me
(Seeing Humans Naked)

In the minds of humans, the most intimate gesture we can offer is
to allow another being to see us naked as a jaybird. It's considered a
special privilege. That's because, as a general rule, most humans not
employed in the adult-entertainment industry have a natural resistance to strutting their junk in front of others. It's called shame and it
dates back to Adam and Eve. As recently as the nineteenth century, a
man and woman could live together for decades without ever seeing
one another's business equipment. Yet, even in those dark Victorian

days of mechanically tightened underwear and blindfolds worn in the shower to prevent accidental glimpses of one's own happy parts, dogs were perfectly welcome in the boudoir.

Why? Probably because, for humans, there is a level of comfort in letting a dog see them naked. Which may be due to the fact that dogs tend not to laugh out loud, snicker, and point at humans, so they assume dogs are not judging them.

However, there is an *honorary* element to the sharing of the nakedness:

SIXTH COMMAND

THY DOG SHALL BE GIVEN SPECIAL PRIORITY CLEARANCE TO SEE THEE NAKED. THIS PRIVILEGE SHALL SUPERSEDE THAT OF LOVERS, BFFS, GYNECOLOGISTS, AND AIRPORT SECURITY PERSONNEL.

Dogs are happy to join their humans for the removing of the clothes, but they don't really get what it's all about. In fact, the whole ritual seems to make dogs just a tad uncomfortable. Not because of the sexual aspect, but for something much more basic: Dogs don't understand the concept of detachable body parts. In other words, dogs can't remove their paws or step out of their fur or hang their ears up to dry. They think of our clothes as *human fur* and our shoes as *human feet*, so when we remove these items in front of them, they get a little nervous, possibly thinking thoughts like these:

❧ *Wha? Whoa! Why is that human taking herself apart?!*

❧ *What does this human want me to do with that pile of spare body parts*

he dropped on the floor there? Bury them? Eat them? Sleep on them? Pee on them? Guess I can try that.

❧ *I'm not sure I like the insides of the human. In fact, I'll say it: 'Eeewww, gross!'*

Adding parts to humans can be just as disturbing to dogs. For example, when someone bursts into the house, dressed in a fright wig and giant shoes, ready to take the dog to the Halloween pet parade, the dog may not be thinking, *Yay, it's party time!* but something more along the lines of *What the eff?! Evil intruder at twelve o'clock . . . must attack.* Or *Holy crap, I've got to run and hide!* In response, the human laughs at the dog's inability to recognize him. This demoralizing laugh can ultimately lead to "the finding of the poop in the slippers" scenario.

Doggie Style vs. Human Style

Dogs also are given special dispensation to watch humans during their mating rituals. When joining humans in the bedroom, dogs tend to lie there on the floor, looking watchful but vaguely stressed, as if they're observing someone trying to insert a helium balloon into a keyhole.

Could this be because humans often do the deed "human-style," as opposed to doggie-style? The dog probably views this approach as, at the very least, *misguided.* This opinion is shared by many humans, who harbor an intense desire to do it doggie-style. In fact, for many humans, the opportunity to . . . um, "engage with one another in a canine posture" is longed for with near religious fervor. (It's like church: Some never go there, some go every day, some go only Sunday, and some go only on holidays and special occasions.) Perhaps this is why they like having the dog in the bedroom. It's a handy way to "casually" bring the idea up with a partner.

The dog probably *worries* about the humans when they're locked in a face-to-face posture. After all, if they are lying there with their fronts smashed into each other, how can they both keep an eye out for squirrels, food items, or balls to chase? Dogs never do it human-style, do they? Tough to picture a female dog lying on her back, bored, waiting for her partner to finish, looking longingly at the cigarettes on the nightstand. So when a dog sees humans mating that way, maybe a part of it wants to shake its head in disbelief the same way it does when humans flush their wonderful autobiographies (poo) down the toilet. Perhaps Dog's presence in the bedroom is a gentle reminder to "do it right," for Dog's sake.

The Sharing of the Bed

No talk of bedroom rituals would be complete without discussing the literal sharing of the bed. While some humans draw a firm line at allowing their dog into bed with them, for other humans that line is about as firm as the spaghetti in a four-year-old can of Chef Boyardee. In short, the dog owns the bed.

SEVENTH COMMAND

WHEN A DOG IS SLEEPING IN THE MIDDLE OF THY BED, THOU SHALT RETREAT TO A NEUTRAL CORNER OF THE MATTRESS AND WILL ALLOW THYSELF TO LAPSE INTO A STATE OF MUSCLE PARALYSIS FOR THE REMAINDER OF THE NIGHT SO AS TO AVOID TRIGGERING A RUMBLE OF ANNOYANCE FROM THE DOG.

Many Dogtologists grant their dogs in-bed privileges that they don't even grant to the love of their life or to their own children. The dog is permitted to crowd them all night, camp on top of their legs for hours, and take over their personal space the minute they get up to go to the bathroom. When trying to move the dog back

to his "own" part of the bed after a trip to the bathroom, the human is often dismayed to discover that the twenty-pound dog suddenly weighs 132 pounds. The human is greeted by a huff of annoyance from the sleeping dog, which the human interprets as a warning that he is pushing his luck. Where do you think the expression "Let sleeping dogs lie" comes from?

x. Holiday Rituals

One of humanity's oddest customs is our tendency to express emotions abstractly, rather than directly, and to do so only on designated holidays. This must seem strange to dogs. Instead of constantly jumping up and licking each other in the face and/or crotch, we hold our emotions in check, then, on special days of the year, go to the store and buy cards (written by other humans) to tell friends and relatives we love them. Instead of wagging our butts till we pee with joy, we hoard our gratitude till Thanksgiving Day, then eat till we explode. Instead of giving generously of ourselves every day of the year, we store up our generosity till Christmas, when we let it loose like a cluster bomb, to the tune of a $3,200 American Express bill.

These holiday rituals would probably be dismissed by Dog as yet another example of incomprehensible human behavior, except for the fact that we insist on *involving* dogs in them. Though these holidays have nothing to do with dogs, we want our dog to be a centerpiece of the festivities. This can include . . .

❋ buying the dog holiday treats from the local gourmet "barkery" in shapes such as paws, bones, curly tails, and dog heads (because nothing says "Happy Holidays" like symbolic cannibalism)

❋ getting the dog groomed and dyed in festive holiday ways (you can practically *hear* the dog sing "tie-de-diddle-de-dee" with hearty Irish cheer as you pull it out of the vat of green dye for St. Patty's Day)

- taking the dog to parades, parties, outdoor concerts, and other noisy, crowded, costume-intensive events that are seemingly designed to overstimulate, frighten, and confuse canines

- coaxing the terrified dog out from under the coffee table to "enjoy" the fireworks display with the family

EIGHTH COMMAND

NOT ONLY SHALT THOU PURCHASE GIFTS *FOR* DOG, FOR BIRTHDAYS AND ALL MAJOR HOLIDAYS, THOU SHALT ALSO BUY GIFTS FOR THYSELF *FROM* DOG AND ACT GENUINELY SURPRISED WHEN THOU OPENEST THEM.

Some dogs seem to dig human holidays. Others seem to hate them. Others just want to zone out and take a nap. But what do they *think* of all our strange holiday rituals? Is it just a freak show for them? A chance to observe us and wonder how they ever got mixed up with us?

Dogs must be especially confused by our habit of storing up emotions only to release them on specified days. They must notice how this habit tends to result in manic behaviors such as dancing on tables with our pants buckled around our head to "ring in the new year" as well as psychiatric meltdowns when designated "joyous" holidays fail to generate the expected level of joy.

XI. Uniforms

The Barking at / Chasing after / Mauling of the Man in the Uniform is an age-old ritual enacted by canines, which forever mystifies Man. No matter how peaceful a dog's disposition, one thing is surer than death, taxes, and the fact that a four-foot-tall, ninety-eight-year-old man in a fedora—driving seven miles per hour in a 1962 Ford Fairlane—will appear ahead of you on the road if you are late for an appointment: Dogs *will* chase after a uniformed human. And they will do so with a focus and ferocity typically displayed by plague-infested zombies in a post-apocalyptic video game.

This ritual baffles humans, yet dogs do not react to *all* uniforms with equal vigor. Experiments reveal, for instance, that nurses are spared from canine rage. So are baseball players, school kids, chefs (for obvious reasons), cowboys, pirates, Indian chiefs, swamis, bagpipe players, and cheerleaders. Doctors are actually *avoided* by dogs (probably due to the fact that they look like veterinarians), and pizza delivery guys are welcomed with open paws. While females, as a general rule, are given a friendly pass, males (specifically males in quasi-military uniforms) cause dogs to go berserk. That includes postal workers, UPS and FedEx guys, police officers, firefighters, airline pilots, park rangers, Civil War reenactors, and, sadly, Cub Scouts.

So, why are males in quasi-military outfits singled out for canine hostility? Could it be that, as with most "bad" dog habits, humankind taught them to attack men in uniform and drilled it into their DNA? Consider this: After centuries of using dogs as our castle guardians and fellow soldiers, perhaps we have genetically conditioned them to become aggressive toward men who look like enemy militia marching onto our turf. Just a thought.

XII. Other Rituals of Dogs and Humans

There are many other enduring rituals both species engage in that cause massive befuddlement on the part of the other species.

Miscellaneous Dog Rituals Humans Don't Get

THE CHASING OF THE CAR

After millennia of breeding dogs to run after large, galloping animals, humans wonder why dogs insist on chasing Impalas, Broncos, and

Mustangs down the street. They might just be following the instincts humans have bred into them, but here's another possibility: Maybe they've become so tired of living with humans that they're willing to run down a carload of complete strangers for a lift out of town. "Hey, wait! Let me in! Take me with you—please!" Can you blame them?

THE STICKING OF THE HEAD OUT THE CAR WINDOW

Man often wonders why Dog is obsessed with sticking his head out the car window. That is perhaps because Man has no idea how bad Man smells, especially to a dog's turbocharged olfactory abilities. Man's underarm sweat glands are among the most odoriferous organs in the entire animal kingdom. Combine this with humans' semi-rancid breath, powerful foot odor, questionable bathroom hygiene, and chemical-smelling deodorant—and with that tree-shaped piece of cardboard dangling from the rearview mirror that we think smells like pine but that a dog thinks smells like exhaust from a nuclear reactor—and it is easy to see why sitting with a group of humans in a hermetically sealed car might prompt a dog to air out its face whenever possible. The wind is literally a breath of fresh air.

THE EATING OF THE GRASS

Why does Dog, the quintessential carnivore, occasionally insist on having a ceremonial dinner of lawn? Answer: If you had to eat 142 bags of Top Dog Pro Plan Calorie-Control kibble in a row, a mouthful of hybrid ryegrass might taste like filet mignon to you, too. Dogs are also smart enough to realize that if their tummy is upset, a few bits of grass will either cure it or make them barf up what's bothering them.

THE SNIFFING OF THE BACK DOOR
(NO . . . THE OTHER "BACK DOOR")

Since the dawn of history, Man has wondered why dogs sniff each other's rumps on a routine basis (whereas humans engage in this behavior only on a single wildly experimental college weekend they spend the rest of their lives trying to forget). Contrary to popular belief, dogs are not just sniffing one another's gas; they are actually sniffing special scent glands that happen to be located in that same area. These glands contain vast amounts of vital information and are, essentially, the dog's private Whizzbook page. Human beings should ponder this the next time they disapprove of a rear-sniff session: Were these scent glands located on the front of the dog, dogs would never have learned to do the Rump-Sniff Daisy Chain, and pack behavior might never have developed in dogs, which means Dog would never have become socialized, which means Dog and Man would never have connected up with each other, which means human civilization would never have advanced beyond the Stone Age. So there.

THE SAMPLING OF THE POO

Even more incomprehensible than posterior sniffing, the Sampling of the Poo is a ritual that has tested the bonds of dog and human like no other (with the friendly lick in the face forever tainted by speculation over where the hell that wet little tongue has just been). DUDs believe doo-doo tasting proves just how "gross" dogs are, but the truth may surprise most humans: Because dog excrement contains so much vital information about a dog, mother dogs learned long ago to bury, hide, or devour their puppy's poo to protect their young from being tracked by dangerous predators. (Once again, what appears to be lowly behavior actually has noble origins. Which raises the natural question: how much do you love *your* kid? Reeeeeeeeeally?)

THE CHEWING OF THE SHOE

Many humans believe that when a dog engages in the ritual Chewing of the Shoe, it demonstrates that the dog is angry or bored because the human left it alone. The real explanation, however, may be simpler. To a dog, shoe leather represents the closest thing to real food it has seen in months. Dogs possess tearing, ripping teeth that need to be exercised regularly but don't get much of a workout eating bowls of kibble pellets that have the consistency of Cap'n Crunch and ingredients one might expect to find in roofing adhesive. Every once in a while the dog feels the need to tear into something of substance, something that once walked the earth on actual biological feet, hooves, or paws, even if that something tastes like Kiwi shoe polish and bears the name Badgley Mischka.

THE STALLING OF THE POOP DROP

This ritual precedes the Evening Crouch and is tied directly to the mood of the human. The way it works is this: The later the hour, the fouler the weather, and the more tired the human, the longer the dog will delay the dropping of the nighttime poop. Why does the dog delay this particular activity? Perhaps to build anticipation in the human so that the actual dropping of the poop is treated with the proper level of solemnity the dog feels it warrants. Or maybe, once again, just because it can.

Miscellaneous Human Rituals Dogs Don't Get

THE RUBBING OF THE NOSE IN THE POOP

The Rubbing of the Nose in the Poop is a reprehensible human ritual that takes place after the human discovers doggie droppings in an undesirable location (i.e., anywhere). When misguided humans engage in this ritual, they are attempting to say to the dog, "Look at what you did! You bad dog, you. *Never* do that again." But what the *dog* is thinking is, *Say whaa? Why is this crazy human randomly charging at me in anger? Why is it grabbing my neck and forcing my face into excrement for no freaking reason?* The dog then associates that particular human with the emotion of fear. And the next time that human enters the room, the dog craps on the floor again. Rinse. Repeat. Rinse. Stupid human.

THE RITUAL SCREAM RESPONSE

Through the years, dogs have learned that certain ritual actions on their part trigger ritual responses from humans. The Barking at the

Man in Uniform, the Chewing of the Shoe, the Sampling of the Poo, and many other canine rituals can be counted on to trigger the Ritual Scream Response from the human. The dog performs the action; the human screams. Like clockwork. The dog finds this response oddly comforting, because it is the one thing about living with humans that is predictable. The dog is thus conditioned to repeat the triggering action many times throughout the day. (It's the reverse of Pavlov's dog: Pavlov's dog's human.)

THE RANDOM TRAINING SESSION

Once or twice per week, Dogtologists feel a need to convince themselves they are "good dog owners" and will roust the dog from its spot on the La-Z-Boy to conduct a Random Training Session. During this ritual, which lasts approximately ten minutes, the human will issue a flurry of verbal commands never heard before by the confused but eager dog, sometimes accompanied by strange hand gestures and random actions such as pressing the dog's butt to the ground and giving it treats. After the ritual ends, the human will proceed to the La-Z-Boy with his bag of Oven Baked Cheetos, the dog will return to its designated position in front of the La-Z-Boy begging for the Oven Baked Cheetos, and life will resume exactly as it was before the ritual, with no observable changes in the canine's (or the human's) behavior.

The goal of Dogtologists is to honor and celebrate Dog. But that goal will never be fully realized until humans are able to create rituals that are more sensitive to the true needs of dogs. That doesn't mean that humans should grab a fork and join the puppy at the litter box, but it does mean they might want to ease off on the doggie leprechaun costumes and green doggie beer. Fair enough? Nah, didn't think so.

I. The Ownership Question: Who Owns Whom? (Or, Who's Whose Bitch?)

Man's relationship with Dog is unique. Yes, humans love their bunnies, ferrets, canaries, turtles, goats, and potbellied pigs, but nothing comes close to the level of devotion Man gives to Dog. YouTube videos of tarantulas wearing tiny sailor caps do not get three million hits on a Tuesday afternoon. Malls do not overflow with stores called Parrot-Phernalia devoted entirely to parrot products. TV networks do not cover the annual Westminster Hermit Crab Show for three days running. Even cats don't get *that* kind of attention, though they come close (Catakism is nearly as widespread as Dogtology).

Oddly, though, even as Dogtologists revere, praise, and celebrate Dog, they also side with DUD culture in one major way: They still regard themselves as *owners* of dogs! "Ownership" of dogs is a strange idea. If dogs really are using Man as a high-level "tool," as some scientists believe, then does it really make sense to say that humans *own* dogs? After all, are *humans* owned by their smartphones? Okay, bad example, but in most cases it is the tool *user* who owns the tool, not the other way around. And since Man is the biggest tool in the known universe, it could easily be argued that dogs are the owners and humans are the possessions.

Legally, sure, a dog is considered a person's property (or in legalese, chattel). But perhaps the fairest statement we can make is that Dog and Man are engaged in a mutually agreed-upon partnership. Neither owns the other. And yet, "dog owner" has become one of those oxymoronic notions, like "smart bomb," "business ethics," "military intelligence," or "airline food," that we have come to accept as reality.

II. The License

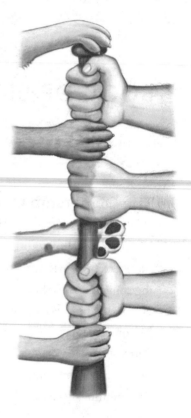

The main symbol of dog ownership (which all "owned" dogs are required by law to display on their collars) is the dog license, or dog tag. When one hears the word "license," the first thing that often comes to mind is a driver's license. Unfortunately, a dog license is nothing like a driver's license.

A driver's license, alas, is a *merit*-based certificate one *earns* after receiving comprehensive training in automobile operation and proving to the state that one is competent to drive a car. One might hope a dog license would be the same: Humans would get trained in canine care and management and would then have to prove that they have the basic skills to be dog owners. But no. Instead, the dog license turns out to be as tough to earn as that other famous human license, the marriage license. While raising a family is arguably the most important task any member of human society can be entrusted with, no training whatsoever is required to obtain a marriage license. None. Zero. Zip. All you're required to produce is a photo ID and, in some states, proof that you're not related to one another, or proof that you've gotten your shots. It's just as easy to get a dog license.

A dog license requires proof of purchase and a rabies certificate. That's all. After these stringent requirements are met, the dog license is duly awarded. Oddly, dogs are the only animal for which a license is required—other than a hunting or fishing license, which permits you to kill the animal specified. There is no cat license, hamster license, sloth license, or bison license (which, by the way, is fun to say).

III. Licensed Dogtologists

For a DUD, the process of getting a dog license is conducted with all the forethought of buying a pack of Duracell batteries at Walgreens. For Dogtologists, however, getting a dog license is a solemn ceremonial event that marks the beginning of a new life. For them, dog "ownership" means taking on a set of responsibilities greater than those of starting a multinational corporation. Believers willingly take on these responsibilities for the privilege of "owning" a dog. It's actually more like a willingness to serve Dog.

Here are just a few things a dedicated dog "owner" must do before and after purchasing—no, no, *uniting* with—a dog:

* Research and select the desired breed.
* Interview and visit dog breeders, if applicable (usually requires travel), or find the nearest rescue facility, so that Dog can save Man once again.
* Shop for and purchase start-up equipment.
* Dog-proof the home.
* Name the dog (an elaborate and time-consuming process—it should be, at least).
* Interview and select the vet.
* House-train.

* Provide behavioral training.

* Feed daily.

* Conduct daily play sessions.

* Manage the kennel club membership, paperwork, and activities.

* Enforce dental hygiene.

* Make regular trips to the groomer.

* Facilitate pooping and peeing excursions several times per day.

* Manage doggie reproduction.

* Make special trips to parks, beaches, and trails.

* Upgrade toys regularly (replacing squeakers as needed).

* Purchase bones from specialty shops (e.g., A Bone to Pick).

   And for deeper Dogtologists . . .

* Snap and upload the doggie photos (constantly).

* Make the doggie-photo Christmas/Hanukkah/Kwanzaa cards.

* Arrange socializing sessions with other dogs and humans.

The number of duties attached to responsible dog ownership would overwhelm Charles Carson, the head butler from *Downton Abbey*. So, of course, the question naturally arises: Why are humans, especially Dogtologists, so willing and eager to invest so much energy in their dogs?

The answer goes to the very heart of Dogtology. . . .

IV. The Payoff

Humans, it turns out, are not fond of investing their effort for no reason. When offered a paycheck at the end of a long workweek, they rarely say, "Nah, you go ahead and keep it. I'm good for now." So why would they willingly take on what amounts to a second full-time job, caring for and raising a dog? Surely there are less labor-intensive hobbies. Like building a three-quarters-scale replica of Mount Rushmore out of beer-can tabs.

Why on earth do they do it? Several possible reasons come to mind: (a) humans are simply hooked on obligation and don't know what to do with their free time; (b) humans need someone who'll love them unconditionally and won't keep a scorecard of favors owed and sins committed; (c) humans just need someone they can boss around (or *think* they can boss around). Or (d) maybe dogs really are *that* bleepin' cute and humans will pay any price to keep them in their lives, even if it means putting the kids in foster care and slapping a second mortgage on the home.

All of these reasons are possible. But perhaps something even deeper is going on here. . . .

There is actually an even greater, unseen payoff that humans get from dog "ownership," something they may not even be consciously aware of: Dogs provide humans with psychological freedoms they are unable to grant themselves. Think about it. Humans, thanks to a little thing Freud called the superego, tend to behave in fearful, repressed, and cautious ways. Humans avoid taking social risks, they stifle their true feelings, and they behave self-consciously the vast majority of the time. But the truth is, they don't *want* to act this way. Deep down, they all want to shed their inhibitions. They all want to be daring lovers and free spirits. They want to run naked in the grass and pour out their gushiest emotions. Their inner child wants to do the mambo!

But, thanks to the superego, it ain't gonna happen.

Being with a dog, though, lets humans kick the superego in the groin. Being with a dog instantly gives them permission to cast off inhibitions and to be bigger and bolder than they normally allow themselves to be. When they're with a dog, humans can strike up a conversation with a stranger on the street. They can throw Frisbees in the park and roll in the grass like a kid. They can shamelessly heap praise on another living thing (the dog). Humans can be goofily, openly loving, gushy, and sentimental.

Dogs give humans license to take all of the best parts of themselves out of mothballs and unleash them on the world. The moment they snap a license onto a dog's collar, they buy *themselves* a license to a bigger, bolder, and more enjoyable life. Isn't that a huge part of why humans love dogs, praise dogs, and admire dogs? Not just for the qualities *dogs* possess, but for the qualities they bring out in *Man*? Turtles don't do that. Gerbils don't do that. Goldfish don't do that. Not the way dogs do.

The license humans get from dogs comes in many forms. . . .

v. License to Flirt

One of the greatest licenses dogs grant humans is the license to hit on other humans. Some humans are naturally flirtatious, but most of them are as adept at it as they are at medieval catapult design. The moment a human spots an attractive fellow human at the grocery store, a nervous signal shoots to their brain that twists their facial muscles into sailors' knots and scrambles their brainwaves. Instead of offering a simple, sincere smile to the cute stranger fondling the cantaloupes, they flash a grimace of torture and blurt out something like "Nice melons" in a choked voice that sounds like Donald Duck gargling pancake syrup, and then they  kick themselves for a week after someone reports them to a manager for being a creep in the produce department. Opportunity smashed. Shame sets in.

But when a dog is involved, it's a different story. Whether both parties have dogs or only one does, the dog gives the humans an easy, nonthreatening way to start a conversation. All potential skeeviness evaporates. The humans now have something fun and cute to focus on: the dog. Dogs can make even scary and threatening situations a breeze. On a dark street at night, for example, a woman might feel nervous to see a man approaching. But not if he has a dog. Now he's Mr. Rogers.

A dog not only *allows* a person to flirt; it practically demands it. A man would look downright silly if he were at the beach and his dog began sniffing out a nice-looking woman's dog and the man didn't engage with the woman. He is *expected* to make conversation. And if he's incapable of following up the encounter with a request for her phone number (the woman's, not her dog's), that's his problem. The dog has done everything in its power to get the guy hooked up.

NINTH COMMAND

WHENEVER THOU EMPLOYEST DOG TO "SCORE" IN A ROMANTIC OR SEXUAL WAY, THOU SHALT REWARDEST THE DOG WITH TREATS MOST SAVORY AND WALKS MOST LENGTHY.

This power, however, comes with a caveat:

There's a reason "Must Love Dogs" is such a popular phrase in the singles pages. Once men and women experience the freedom and ease a dog brings to their dating lives, there's no going back to the awkwardness of dating a human alone.

VI. License to Act Civilized

Dogs not only make it easier for humans to approach would-be *lovers*, but they also give them license to be friendly to *everyone*.

Humans are extremely sociable creatures, deep down, but for some reason they don't always allow this side of themselves to show. Instead, they go around with their heads down, acting as if accidental eye contact with a fellow human might expose them to a deadly gaze-borne contagion. The reason for this behavior is the "douche protocol." The douche protocol mandates that humans must treat their fellow man with rudeness, contempt, suspicion, and general douchiness, unless given a *specific reason not to*. Then, and only then, may a person transform into a Mother Theresa or a George Clooney. For example, the moment a disaster strikes, ordinary humans instantly start showing concern and attention toward others they didn't give a bone about yesterday. That's because humans need a socially acceptable *excuse* to break the douche protocol.

An excellent illustration of this paradigm is Nautical Law.

Nautical Law states that it is perfectly permissible (mandatory, in fact) to act friendly and outgoing toward another human being, provided at least one of the parties is aboard an aquatic vessel. It's a curious thing. We spend years teaching our children to avoid talking to strangers. Unless the stranger is on a boat. Then we virtually *force* our child to wave and smile and jump up and down like an idiot. It can be any kind of boat—sailboat, rowboat, kayak, catamaran—on any sized body of water. Cruise ships are the best—they give us the opportunity to exchange smiles and waves with thousands of strangers all at once.

Why is this? What is it about standing on a boat that suddenly makes every stranger every other human's next new pal? It just *does*. The presence of a boat is simply a mutually agreed-upon excuse to sidestep the douche protocol.

Canine Law

Similarly, the presence of a dog gives Man universal license to ignore the douche protocol. Dogs serve as all-purpose go-betweens. They're social lubricants. They give humans an immediate sense of commonality, safety, and unity with each other, and instant permission to be warm and friendly, as opposed to the traditional "I will loathe you with every judgmental cell in my body until you give me a good reason not to" approach that guides too many human interactions.

It is *always* okay to talk to a dog and, by extension, to the human at the other end of the dog's leash. A dog park is the most extreme example of this. Humans who meet in dog parks immediately begin conversing with one another at a level of intimacy typically reserved for Ethan Hawke / Julie Delpy sequels. A higher being bringing oneness to all.

Note: when Nautical Law and Canine Law come together, as in the case of a cute puppy wearing a life-vest, there is such an explosion of good will that naval warships have been known to spontaneously cease firing.

VII. License to Stomp All Over Taboos

Dog gives Man license to say and do a *whole range* of things that are usually taboo:

Invite oneself to others' homes. Most humans would never think to boldly invite themselves to a home they've never visited, but it's fun and easy when they're setting up a doggie play date! They just say something like, "We've *got* to get our dogs together. I'll drop by your place on Saturday." And it's done.

Ignore property lines. Humans are extremely sensitive about having strange and unknown two-leggeds wander onto their property—unless a dog is present with them. Then the stranger is allowed to follow the pup wherever it wants to wander (as long as the dog does not make a lawn deposit, because then it's War of the Worlds). The stranger can even stop and have a loud cell phone conversation on the homeowner's front lawn for forty-five minutes, provided she is providing a fur fix.

Talk about sex, body fluids, and intimate bodily functions. The presence of dogs allows humans to freely discuss topics that would be unmentionable in polite society. Even among the snooty crowds at Westminster dog shows, one can catch fragments of sentences like "bitches in heat," "keep him on a tight leash," and "bloated ticks"—of course that's when they're discussing dogs, not other humans . . . for the most part.

Yell at the neighbors' kids. Normally, humans go ballistic when other humans correct the behavior of their precious preschoolers. But if a kid pulls a dog's tail or pokes a dog with a stick, then all bets are off. The dog "owner" can freely tear the child a new one while its parents nod in agreement. Protecting Dog is a duty that supersedes parental rights and resuscitates that ancient and forgotten art known as "scolding."

VIII. License to Be Five

One of the coolest licenses dogs give humans is the license to act as if they are five years old.

Scientists tell us that humans and dogs have one special thing in common besides a high gastric tolerance for neon-yellow cheese-food products: their love of play. Most mammals do not share this trait. Play is usually a phase that animals pass through very early in life. Play has a developmental purpose: It teaches the animal certain skills essential for survival. Most mammals quickly outgrow the play phase and settle into an adult life of standing around mooing, obsessing over acorns, or getting flattened by automobiles.

Dogs and humans, however, enjoy play throughout their lives. But there is one key difference between dogs and humans in this regard: Humans pretend to outgrow play; dogs aren't even capable of pretending that. This means that humans must be given *license* to play. Enter Dog. Dogs enjoy many of the same games humans do, such as tag, wrestle in the grass, chase the thing, hide the thing, and chew up the thing.

Playing with a ball, for example, is especially desirable to both humans and dogs. Dogs indulge this desire by . . . playing with a ball.

Humans indulge this desire by hiring other humans to play with balls, sitting on a couch in front of a TV, and watching those humans play with balls, and then reading newspaper analyses about how well their chosen groups of ball players played with their balls yesterday and are scheduled to play with their balls tomorrow.

Somewhere in the process, however, "fun" seems to have gotten left out. Dog changes that. When humans hang out with dogs, they get to yell, shriek, squeal, roll around on the floor, and laugh like toddlers, and nobody judges them for it. They have license to act like monkeys on 'shrooms. Take away the dog, and the same human behaviors would result in emergency psych evaluations.

Humans always say how much dogs love to play ball. Ever wonder if the dog sees the smile on the face of the humans and believes *they* love it? Perhaps Rover goes and gets the ball when Dad gets home because he knows how it clears Dad's mind and refreshes Dad's attitude.

IX. License to Come Back Down to Earth Now and Then

Humans spend all day in front of computers, then come home and spend all evening in front of iPads, iPhones, and TV screens, wandering off to bed in a trance only when their devices need recharging. Many of them know their *World of Warcraft* guild or Farmville neighbors better than they know their own family members. Some of them have many "friends," yes, but those friendships consist of clicking "Like" buttons on Facebook pages. The actual person allegedly being communicated with might have died five years ago and the human wouldn't know it, as long as someone kept logging on to the "friend's" Facebook account and posting comments like "OMG, UR having a blond moment, GF. LMAO!" If these trends continue, human existence will soon become 100 percent virtual.

Dogs give humans license to come back to reality every once in a while. "Reality?" one might ask. "What the heck is that?" It's that place where there are physical things like trees and rocks and streams and birds and other humans. Dogs still *live* in that strange, physical, alternative world, and they give Man license to go there with them. They force humans to smell fresh air, feel unpaved dirt beneath their feet, and hear the wind in the trees. As much as humans hate to put the iPad down, part of them comes alive when they enter this place called reality. Their hearts pump, their skin soaks in rays from a nearby star known as the "sun," and their noses fill with odors created by living things that breathe *real* oxygen and carbon dioxide, just like humans learned about in their fifth-grade science class.

Of course, if humans could find a way to digitize their dogs and load them into laptops so they could hang with them online, they would do so. But since they can't, they settle for the next-best thing. *Reality*. Man has Dog to thank for that.

X. License to Be Sappy and Sentimental

Humans fool themselves in a thousand ways. For example, they like to tell themselves that as they get older they attain a state known as "emotional maturity." In this fantasy state, they supposedly outgrow the sappy sentimentality of childhood and become smarter and more sophisticated in their tastes. *Not!* Truth is, humans are giant emotional saps, but pretend to be mature because everyone else is doing it. Look around a movie theater at the end of a Pixar film and you'll see kids in full diabetic comas from Milk Duds and Coke, but there's not a dry adult eye in the place. As soon as the house lights go on, though, *bam*: instant faux-bored, faux-jaded parents.

Dogs give everyone permission to express their sappiest emotions. The sugary "awwws" that pour out of the puppy wing of the local pet shelter sound like the soundtrack to a film called *The Pink Candy Unicorn Who Found Her Lost Mommy*. Puppies reduce the meanest drill sergeant, the most hardened convict, the most humorless bureaucrat to quivering masses of emotional blubber. Even as dogs age, everyone continues to view them as "cute" and heartwarming. Put a plaque on the wall full of sappy thoughts about doggie love and humans will weep openly. Even DUDs are not immune. Well, not most of them.

With their own dogs, of course, humans allow themselves to express goofily over-the-top love on a constant basis. They make ridiculous sounds in their dogs' faces and force them to endure endless hugging, kissing, and belly raspberrying. They even make up new words for dogs, like "wiggle-snoosh," "poopie-shnoops," and "cuddle-muffin," because the humans' native languages aren't nearly sappy enough to capture the mushiness of their feelings. And without the outlet dogs give humans to vent their sappiness, the entire human race would eventually explode in a repressed mass of gooey syrup and Hallmark card poetry.

XI. License to Intimidate

Not all of the licenses granted to Man by Dog are soft and mushy. Dogs also give humans the license to kick butts and take names. Dogs can instill instant fear and turn human gastrointestinal systems into pureed spinach.

When someone says, "Call in the dogs," it means they're getting down to business. No more screwing around. Dogs are brought in to do stuff like find escaped convicts, locate dead bodies, collect crime evidence, sniff out drugs in lockers and suitcases, attack and subdue the enemy, find bombs, locate stolen property, and fend off angry mobs. When the dogs are brought in, it means the humans have given it their best shot and have failed; now it's time to *get the job done*. It means if someone is guilty of something, they are about to get caught; if they are lost, they are about to get found; and if they are somewhere they're not supposed to be, they are about to get enthusiastically relocated—minus a chunk of their upper thigh.

Okay, recap:

Question: When do humans call in the dogs?

Answer: When they need the superior senses of dogs or want to look tough, cool, threatening, or serious.

Question: When do dogs call in the humans?

Answer: When the dog craps on the floor and needs someone to clean it up.

That pretty much sums it up.

XII. License to Get Out of Dodge

One of the greatest gifts Dog gives Man is an all-purpose get-out-of-jail-free license that allows Man to weasel out of virtually any situation he doesn't feel like dealing with. Dogs give humans a handy excuse to turn down invitations, cancel plans at the last minute, and cut out of events early.

The following generic dog excuses have been known to be used effectively, even on DUDs:

* "I need to go home so I can let my dog out to pee."

* "My dog has an appointment with the vet."

* "I need to go walk my dog."

* "My dog isn't feeling well. I need to keep an eye on her."

* "My dog sitter canceled on me at the last minute. Can you *believe* that?!"

* "I need to pick my dog up at the groomer's."

* "My dog's choking on a chicken bone! Call you right back!"

* And the most famous one of all: "My dog ate my homework! *AAARRGGHH!*"

The following excuses, on the other hand, tend to work best with fellow Dogtologists (who understand dog devotion and tend to cut one another a lot more slack):

- "My dog suffers from seasonal affective disorder and shouldn't be alone on a cloudy day."

- "My dog's chakras are out of alignment and need retuning."

- "My dog just won the Cutest Dog in the World Award and I've got to go pick up her prize."

- "My neighbor has rabies and I'm afraid my dog is going to bite him and get sick."

- "I need to talk to my dog about drugs. I can't put it off any longer."

- "My dog just attained enlightenment and I have to spend some time in his aura."

XIII. The Power of the Pups

Lastly, dogs just seem to give humans license to . . . well, be human.

In the eighties film *Starman*, an alien who has spent some time on planet Earth says to a human, "You are a strange species. . . . Shall I tell you what I find beautiful about you? You are at your very best when things are worst."

He doesn't mention the other side of the coin: that on any average given day, humans are at their very worst. They go around being angry, critical, suspicious, stingy, jealous, fearful, defensive, intolerant, and judgmental 98 percent of the time. And yet, give them the slightest excuse to flip the switch and suddenly they're tickling babies and singing "We Are the World."

They can't seem to flip the switch on their own, though. They need some kind of catalyst. Or *dog*alyst, to be more precise. Dogs give humans permission, on a daily basis, to be better versions of themselves—fun loving, caring, and compassionate. And humans *love* that version of themselves. So they love dogs for bringing it out in them. Potbellied pigs and baby chicks may be cute, but they don't have the *power of the pups* to flip the switch. Only dogs seem able to do that.

I. Canine Realization

A Canine Realization is the moment a human realizes that she is truly a believer. It is the moment she knows that she needs Dog in her life even more than she needs . . . Facebook. Experiencing the Canine Realization can bring a feeling of great exhilaration, but also soberness, because from the moment one *owns* one's belief in Dogtology, one's life forever changes. One begins to feel not only *okay* about one's pants pockets carrying the indelible scent of Waggin' Wheels Freeze Dried Chicken Livers and one's car upholstery having enough fur on it to pass for sheepskin seat covers, but also *proud* of such things, and one begins to openly boast about those traits.

A Canine Realization typically occurs under one of three scenarios.

Coming Out of the Closet

Sometimes a person is a "closet Dogtologist." That is, they've been practicing Dogtology for years, in thought, word, and deed, but simply haven't realized it, have been living in denial, or haven't even known that something called Dogtology exists. Then one day the truth dawns and they suddenly know what and who they are. They no longer wish to hide it from themselves or the world. The moment they admit the truth about themselves, it's like the Scarecrow getting his "brains" in *The Wizard of Oz*. They realize Dogtology was inside them all along. This can lead to a difficult conversation with one's parents, especially if they are DUDs. "Mom . . . Dad . . . I need to talk to you about something. I've been having these . . . *feelings* and I can't hide who I am anymore . . ."

TENTH COMMAND

IF THOU CLAIMETH NOT TO REVERE DOGS, BUT HEARETH THYSELF SAYING TO A HOUND, "COME TO DADDY AND SEE THE YUMMY RIB-EYE STEAK HE GRILLED FOR YOU," FACE IT, THOU ART A DOG-TOLOGIST. COME OUT OF THE CLOSET ALREADY!

Graduation

Sometimes a garden-variety dog *enthusiast* graduates to a whole new level of dog love and becomes a certified *apostle*. Many find themselves in this boat. They enjoy dogs but aren't obsessed with them. And then suddenly, one day, something changes. It's like the moment when a human romantic relationship flips from *I think I like this person* to *I love this person. I can't live without this person. I must be with this person 24/7 and get a custom-built bobblehead doll made of this person so I can put it in the bathroom and never be away from this person.*

It can be a single experience that pushes a dog fancier into becoming a full-blown Dogtologist, or it can be the result of steady growth and evolution. Many "dog people" do not start out as Dogtologists, just as most first-time wine drinkers don't rush out and buy a case of

1978 Henri Jayer Richebourg Grand Cru to start their collection. It happens in stages.

Age is often a factor, as well. The older humans grow, and the more jaded they become by experiencing the constant ups and downs of human relationships, the better Dog starts to look to them. The day eventually comes when the simple love and adoration for dogs becomes an essential part of one's core, and getting a daily fur fix becomes a must.

Spontaneous Enlightenment

Sometimes DUDs suddenly and unexpectedly become Dogtologists. This is similar to the spontaneous spiritual enlightenment that death-row inmates or hikers lost in the wilderness sometimes experience. The DUD may have told himself all his life that he doesn't like dogs. Perhaps he had a bad experience with a dog as a child, which shut down his inner canine receptors. Then one day as an adult he is forced by fate to spend time with a dog. At first he resists the dog mightily, but the dog turns on the extra cuteness. The DUD's resistance begins to slip. He finds himself "casually" carrying dog treats in his pocket. He notices that whenever the dog leaves the room, his hands start shaking. He has cold sweats and heart palpitations. When the dog returns, he begins rolling on the floor with it, laughing hysterically, telling the dog to stop licking him, while doing absolutely nothing to prevent it. He's hooked. By the next weekend he's skulking around dog shelters in a trench coat and shades, asking if anyone knows where he can score some high-quality Labrador.

II. The Catalyst Dogalyst

Just as there are various types of Canine Realization, there are also various triggers, or catalysts dogalysts, that can push a person toward having a Canine Realization. Here are just a few:

Doggie Need

Humans often take dogs for granted until the moment they really and truly *need* them. This sometimes happens when a human goes through a difficult struggle in life and a dog is the only one there to listen. It can happen when a person is lost or injured and is forced to depend on a dog for rescuing or protection. It can happen when a human is home alone at night and realizes he is counting on a dog to make him feel safe.

It can also happen with somebody who is trying to lose twenty pounds and needs a true friend to remove the temptation of that cheesy bacon casserole sitting on the counter. Bam, temptation removed! "Thanks, Patches, for taking one for the team!"

Doggie Deprivation

In a similar way, the loss of a dog, whether temporary or permanent, can move a closet Dogtologist, or even a DUD, to an acceptance of his or her dog addiction.

Perhaps the dog needs to spend a couple of days at the animal hospital or escapes from home and goes missing. The sudden absence of the dog for even a few hours, and the fear of never seeing it again, is enough to burn away all pretenses of DUDliness and drive one to one's knees, praying for doggie deliverance.

Sometimes even the slightest doggie deprivation, such as Peaches being away at a grooming appointment, can be enough to make the human feel the aching void left in the home by the absence of Dog. Sometimes it takes the most profound sacrifice of all, the death of a dog, before a person fully *gets* the need for Dog. When a great dog dies, and they're all great, it can push even a dyed-in-the-wool DUD into an acceptance of Dogtology and a desire to repent for committing the Seven DUDly Sins. Sometimes, alas, loss is the only way to break through to Man's heart.

Doggie Heroism

One of the most dramatic ways a person attains realization is by witnessing a dog performing an act of heroism—rescuing a baby from a burning building, protecting its owner from assault, swimming through stormy seas to save a drowning person. To dogs, these acts are simply known as "being a dog"; dogs don't seem to get what the big deal is. It is humans who find them so newsworthy. It says a lot about humans that they feel a need to throw parades for themselves whenever they do anything resembling the way a dog acts naturally.

It is especially telling to watch how Dog and Man behave *after* an act of heroism. After a dog rescues a toddler from a fire, for example, he curls up in the corner and scratches himself. It's just another day at the office. After a human rescues a toddler from a fire, however, he whips out a mirror, combs his hair, and gets ready for the *News at Five* camera crew to interview him, then starts looking for an agent to shop the rights to his life story.

Still, it is undeniable that the courage and selflessness of a dog can transform many from DUD to fanatical believer in a literal heartbeat.

Doggie Love at First Sight

Sometimes all it takes is "just one look" from *the* dog—the canine love of one's life—and a human is hooked forever. The human walks into a pet store or shelter "just to browse" and wanders over to a certain pup, its tail wagging, and the human just *knows*. He *must* have that dog, even if that means selling his penthouse condo and moving into a ground unit at the Dump View Trailer Park. Any practical issue that stands in the way of the human "owning" that dog (say, the fact that his mate has a lethal allergy to dogs) is instantly forgotten. An immediate and eternal bond is formed between the human and the dog, which converts him from a casual dog lover to a raving Dogtologist in a single moment worthy of a soundtrack the likes of "Wind Beneath My Wings."

III. Reading the Signs

How do you know for sure that you have become a Dogtologist? Sometimes just looking at your life with fresh eyes can be enough to confirm it: Returning home after vacation and being able to see (and smell) your living space objectively. Noticing the rack of seven dog leashes, each with a specific, fine-tuned purpose that only you know. Smelling the odor of wet dog ingrained in the $2,000 sofa that only weeks ago was to be off limits to the pup. Examining the huge "doggie entertainment center" in the middle of the living room, complete with doggie ropes, treadmill, and doggie swing, which has forced your own TV into storage. Navigating the drifted piles of bones and dog toys covering all the heating vents and baseboards. Admiring the fine canine tooth-work engraving the legs of every piece of wooden furniture. These are all signs that a crazy person lives in this home. And that crazy person is *you*.

What's more, you love it.

Once you have experienced a Canine Realization, the next step is true acceptance of your belief. Realization and acceptance are two different things, as any person who has received a diagnosis from a frowning doctor knows. While a Canine Realization can happen in an instant, true acceptance is a slower process that requires time, honesty, courage, moral humility, and fearless self-examination. (Joining a support group may be necessary.)

Barktism?

Perhaps one day the acceptance of Dogtology will be marked by a formal ritual, called a barktism. This barktism might involve the ceremonial dunking of the human's head in a dog's water dish before a congregation of the faithful, as vows of commitment are recited and songs of Dog are sung.

But for now, Dogtologists must be content to mark their faith with a less formal version of the barktism: that pivotal moment when we first allow ourselves to be soaked from head to toe in the enthusiastic saliva of a licking dog—and not wipe it off. The barktism, formal or informal, marks the surrender of all resistance to Dog and the beginning of a new life of complete acceptance and reverence.

IV. The Twelve Stages of Acceptance

In becoming a Dogtologist, one typically progresses through twelve identifiable stages.

1 Admit you are powerless over your doggie obsession.

2 Come to believe that a greater power can restore you to sanity (oddly enough, however, it is the same power with which you were obsessed in the first place: Dog!).

3 Make a decision to turn your life over to the praising of Dog, in whatever form you understand him to be (Chihuahua, Labrador, malamute, terrier, etc.).

4 Humbly ask Dog to forgive you for any shortcomings you may have manifested in your relationship with dogs, offering him pepperoni under the table as restitution.

5 Prepare to have Dog help you remove all of these defects of character (and ask him, while he he's at it, to remove that raw egg you just dropped on the floor).

6 Vow to continue to take personal inventory of your shortcomings (as well as inventory of kitchen cabinets, doggie toy boxes, and glove compartments, and to promptly restock all doggie treats and toys).

7 Seek to improve your conscious contact with Dog, understanding that this might require you to occasionally stop making noise with your own face and actually pay attention to what Dog wants.

8 Promise to unapologetically display the outward signs of Dogtology, including gaudy and tasteless plaques, posters, and bumper stickers bearing messages such as "My windows aren't dirty, that's my dog's nose art," "That's why they call it FUR-niture," and "Dear Dog, please make sure your owner is on a leash."

9 Promise to love, honor, and obey Dog, from this day forward till death do you part (even on days when you come home from work and all the stuffing is ripped out of the sofa and Dog is the only one who could have done it but he's acting all, "What? Me? You think *I* did this?").

10 Make a fearless moral inventory of yourself, asking whether you are guilty of committing any of the Seven DUDly Sins.

11 Admit the exact nature of the Seven DUDly Sins you've committed.

12 Make a list of all dogs you have committed DUDly sins against and be willing to make amends to them (or at least to carry a pocketful of Liv-a-Snaps for all dogs from this day forward).

V. Practical Considerations for Dogtologists

Accepting Dogtology into one's life is not without its challenges. Being obsessively devoted to a furry, attention-loving, four-legged, lap-seeking missile requires certain lifestyle adjustments and compromises. After all, if a Dogtologist is spending roughly 95.2 percent of their life walking their dog, playing with their dog, cuddling with their dog, taking pictures of their dog, sleeping with their dog, shopping for their dog, feeding their dog, taking their dog to appointments, talking about dogs, looking at YouTube videos of dogs on skateboards, and reading dog blogs, something's gotta give. And that something is usually their fellow man (followed closely by their home, their career, and their finances).

Here are some practical issues that must be considered when taking one's Dogtology out into the world.

Declaring One's Faith

Once one has had a Canine Realization, it is important to be candid with other human beings about one's Dogtological beliefs. This is especially true if one is in a committed relationship with another human, or plans to be. For instance, just as it would be unfair to omit mentioning, until after one's wedding, that one is an orthodox

THE SEVEN DUDLY SINS

RENEGING ON A PROMISE OF A WALK

REMOVING A SLEEPING DOG FROM A
BED OR SOFA

FAILING TO DELIBERATELY DROP SCRAPS
DURING FOOD PREPARATION

USING THE VACUUM CLEANER, EVER,
AT ANY TIME

STOPPING A DOG'S BUTT SCOOTCH WHILE
IN PROGRESS—ESPECIALLY WHEN VISITORS
ARE IN THE ROOM

BUYING A COVERED (I.E. SNACK-PROOF)
LITTER BOX

DOING THE FAKE BALL THROW

fundamentalist who is only permitted to make love through a hole in a plastic sheet sprayed with disinfectant, it would also be unfair to hide one's doggie devotion from prospective partners. After all, "normal" humans might reasonably expect to be able to do things like own valuable objects (without teeth marks), live in a clean-smelling home, go out to eat as a couple at an indoor restaurant (not just as a threesome), and possess something called disposable (i.e., post-canine) income. And of course, none of these things are possible if one is a true follower. The Dogtologist doesn't mind this lifestyle, but the partner may not have signed on for this.

Intermarriage

It is generally recommended that Dogtologists marry within their own faith. This is not for moral reasons, but for practical ones. Just as it would be difficult for a hardcore vegan to have a happy, peaceful relationship with a practicing cannibal, it is tricky for nonbelievers to live with Dogtologists. Someone has to back down when it comes to dog-related decisions, and that someone is never the Dogtologist. Though DUDs tend to cut Dogtologists a fair amount of slack, *living* with them is another matter.

Here are just a few of the many intermarrying scenarios that can occur:

Dogtologist marries DUD. Dogtologists sometimes end up married to DUDs. As long as the DUD has a generally tolerant attitude toward dogs, shows some potential for rehabilitation, and agrees to do everything the Dogtologist's way, this kind of relationship can work. Possibly. For a while. Eventually, however, there will be an argument in which the DUD makes the mistake of saying, "It's either me or the dog!" (and immediately begins to experience the joys of Match.com).

Dogtologist marries dog *hater*. This combo is not possible. A dog hater does not get a second date with a Dogtologist. Period. End of relationship. End of story. The hater is advised to leave immediately or, depending upon how delicately the hater's doggie disdain has been stated, to call an ambulance while the Dogtologist looks for the carving knife.

Dogtologist marries extreme Dogtologist. As with any belief system, there are many levels of intensity within the Dogtology faith. It is not unusual for a Dogtologist to marry a fellow Dogtologist only to learn, after the house sharing starts, that the partner is more of an extremist than first realized. "Oh . . . so you two *share* the ice cream, do you? Out of the same doggie dish? Right down there on the floor? Hmm. Wow. Awesome. Wow. Hey, listen," she says, glancing at her wristwatch, "I just remembered—I'm supposed to go visit my cousin in Schenectady for the next couple of decades."

Dogtologist marries Dogtologist of a different sect. Sometimes two Dogtologists can hook up only to discover upon marriage that they belong to very different branches of Dogtology. One might be in the Paint My Precious's Nails a Different Color for Every Day of the Week sect, while the other might be in the Go All Survivalist in the Woods with My Dog Bro sect. Both have an equal love of dogs, but the love manifests itself in such different ways that the only sane option for the dog is to run away and join the circus.

Dogtology and Children

One of the most agonizing decisions a Dogtologist must make is whether to have (human) children. Often Dogtologists do not feel the need to have kids, because caring for their dog more than satisfies their parental urges. In fact, they often call themselves Mommy and Daddy to their dog. But eventually, pressures from spouse, parents, peers, society, and a ticking biological clock begin to mount and the Dogtologist is forced, under duress, to take the issue of human children into consideration. (Note that many municipalities have "no questions asked" laws that allow one to turn in one's offspring without penalty at a fire station, police station, or hospital, if they are under a certain age. Inquire as to age restrictions in your jurisdiction.)

Many Dogtologists, especially women, secretly fear having children because of two possible outcomes, both of which are utterly horrifying to her: (1) She might discover that she can love something more than her precious pup, or (2) even worse, she might discover that she can't. Both possibilities, in her mind, make her the Worst Human Being in the Galaxy. Which can tend to dampen her maternal instincts just a tad.

If a Dogtologist couple does decide to have human children, the question naturally arises: "Shall we raise our child within the Dogtology faith?" The answer, of course, is yes. Dogtologists with children are advised to treat the dog as a full family member and include it in all family activities, including weddings and funerals. That way, the child will grow up revering dogs and will naturally become a believer, without any need for *indogtrination*. More importantly, if the dog is included in everything, the child will never have to see what would happen if her parents were forced to choose between the child and the dog. (And neither will you, Mommie dearest, neither will you.)

Nonpracticing Dogtologists

A Dogtologist's love of Dog and commitment to Dog never changes, so there are no "lapsed" or "former" Dogtologists (as there are with other faiths). There may, however, be times in life when, due to temporary circumstances, it is not possible for a Dogtologist to have a dog. Perhaps the Dogtologist is in mourning following the loss of a dog. Perhaps the Dogtologist is going through a divorce and trying to resolve dog custody issues. Perhaps the Dogtologist is temporarily living in a situation where dogs are not allowed, such as on the Green Mile or on a manned mission to Mars. In cases like these, without an actual dog to obsess over, the temporarily nonpracticing Dogtologist runs the risk of being mistaken for sane. *Great care must be taken to avoid this!* That is why it is important, even when one does not currently have a dog, to continue to keep up appearances:

- Wallpaper one's office cubicle with pictures of dogs, known and unknown.

- Be seen visiting dog parks, alone, just to get a fur fix.

- Stop in at shops like Howlistic Foods, Doggie Styles, and dog pickup joints such as Yo Yo Beeotch, just to say hi to the staff and keep your retail relationships current.

- Forward a minimum of four YouTube dog videos per week to everyone on your contacts list and continue to send dog-themed cards for every holiday and birthday.

- Invite your friends' and family's *dogs* over for the weekend (but not your friends and family).

In this way, when an actual dog once again owns you, no one will be surprised or blindsided by the depth of your obsession—oops, your *faith*.

Reconciling Dogtology with Other Faiths

Many Dogtologists are official members of other beliefs and religions. This is perfectly fine. Dogtology does not require one to make an either/or choice. However, there are certain issues that can create religious tension within a Dogtologist. For example, a debate has raged since the dawn of civilization as to whether dogs have a soul. The official answer, from most religions, has been a resounding, "NO, BLASPHEMER, DAMN YOU TO THE DEPTHS OF HADES FOR EVEN SUGGESTING SUCH A THING!" However, the answer from most Dogtologists has been a resounding "What are you, bleepin' *kidding* me? Of *course* they have a soul, moron!"

For believers, all it takes is one look into the eyes of a dog to clear the issue up once and for all. Though Dogtologists do try to follow the dogma of their *official* temples and churches, no Dogtologist can really get behind the whole "dogs have no soul" thing, no matter what anyone says. The truth is, it is the *soul* of Dog, more than anything else, that turns otherwise normal humans into Dogtologists. There, said it.

VI. It's Dog's World

Whatever one thinks about its adherents, Dogtology is a movement that cannot be stopped. It has been gathering steam for centuries and has now reached critical mass. It is too big to be stuffed under the rug any longer. Just look around. When a tourist town can no longer support a bookstore but *can* support four shops devoted to dog gifts, natural dog foods, dog fitness, and dog baked goods, something extraordinary is happening. When a pet oncologist can offer a $6,000 state-of-the-art course of chemotherapy for dogs, and humans are willing to pay it in order to spend an extra six months with their dogs, a true movement is afoot. When doggie hotels, doggie funeral parlors, and doggie therapy centers stop being movie punch lines and become legitimate real-world businesses, the time has come to shout this thing from the rooftops.

Dogtology. Say it loud and say it proud!

Dogtologists have done everything but build temples to Dog, but maybe that's as it should be. If humans had to go to a separate place to "worship" Dog, it would feel too separate. We would never allow dogs to be so distant from our lives, even in an intellectual way. We need our devotion to be close at hand.

And so our homes, offices, cars, and yards have become the real temples to Dogtology. Here is where we display our plaques, statues, and images of Dog. Here is where we keep our endless supply of leashes and collars and costumes, novelties, gadgets, toys, and flea elixirs. The "temple" of Dogtology is the world we've created around us in devotion to Dog.

Dog is our everyday "deity."

Why is it so important to acknowledge and accept Dogtology? It's all about being straight with oneself. The truth shall set ye free! By openly admitting to being Dogtologists, believers can begin to live more honest and balanced lives. They can begin to factor

Dogtology into their decision-making processes, which will cause them to be fairer and kinder to everyone involved. For example, they will no longer fool themselves into doing things like entering into a long-term relationship with a hopeless DUD, taking a sixty-hour-a-week job that eats into their dog time, moving to a town that lacks good dog parks and dog trails, or trying to have a savings account. True believers can now put Dogtology first, where it belongs, and be proud of it. They need no longer allow side distractions like careers and families to trick them into thinking that dogs are just a hobby. They can *own* their obsession and build a life around it.

That's not too much to ask for a being that brings so much joy into the world, now, is it?

DOGTOLOGY! *Howl-elujah!*

IN THE END

(Which Is Really the Beginning) . . .

Did it really take reading this book for you to figure out how much you believe in me?

Really? You knew it all along, I suspect, but were afraid to admit it.

There's something I want to say to you while I still have your attention. And I have to use words this time, not just my usual barks and growls. So here it goes . . .

Do me a favor, will you? Step outside for a minute on the next clear night. Look up at the night sky. See that big sparkly . . . *thing* up there? That's called "the universe." Pretty awesome, eh?

Okay, now look for the shiniest object you can find. That's Sirius, the Dog Star. That's what you humans named your brightest star (no accident there). Now look upward from Sirius and try to spot Orion the hunter. That represents you: Man—women and men. And right by your side are your two dogs, Canis Major and Canis Minor, the big dog and the little dog. Protecting you and keeping you safe. Do you see me yet? There I am, forever by your side, bright and shiny as can be. Doing things your way. Obeying your rules and doing the jobs you ask of me. Going for walks when you want, watching your TV shows, and eating the "food" you choose for me.

It has taken thousands of years, but many of you are finally starting to wake up to the fact that I'm more to you than just a silent partner. You're becoming true believers. I look around your homes and I see pictures of me where you used to put pictures of your grandparents and your nation's leaders. Little statues of me, too, and moving pictures of me on your glowing screens. When you're away from me I notice that you seek constant reminders of my love for you, in the form of doggie stickers and doggie coffee mugs and doggie T-shirts. So I know you're waking up. Of course, you're doing so in your slow, awkward, human way (FYI, the sooner we get past the Bowser Beer and Poochie Pants stage, the better), but you're finally starting to get what I really am to you:

Your champion!

Your confidant!

Your honest-to-goodness, lay-down-my-life-for-you partner!

Your very best friend!

I've always been here for you, watching over you, accepting you, giving you loyalty, loving you unconditionally—even with your dirty socks and your loud machines.

Loving you.

Forgiving you.

Believing in you.

Through thick and thin.

Awake and asleep.

Till death do us part.

Isn't it time you tried to see things through my eyes just a little? I mean *really* tried. Not just putting your thoughts and tastes in my head and calling them mine? When you finally figure out how to do that, you'll be in for a big surprise. There's a lot more to me than you've even begun to suspect . . .

But for starters . . . enough with the foam antlers already. Seriously.

Thanks, Man. Who's a good human? *You're* a good human, yes you
are, yes you are.

XOXO
Dog

FURMINOLOGY

barktism. A ritual of commitment to Dogtology that new Dogtologists may one day soon choose to undergo. May involve ceremonial facial dunking in a dog's water dish or full body immersion in dog slobber—sometimes by accident.

Book of Fleas. The controversial lost book of Dogtology (containing the Eleventh Command), believed to have been lost in the Great Flea Bath of 519 AD (After Dog).

Canine Law. A social rule that states, "Any human walking a dog shall be instantly deemed trustworthy and suitable for intimate conversation." Canine Law cancels out the douche protocol.

Canine Mensa Society. An elite association made up of the world's most intelligent dogs, of which all Dogtologists privately believe their dog is president, chairpup, and founder.

Canine Realization. The specific moment in time one becomes consciously aware that one is a Dogtologist.

canine-ization. (1) The "doggification" of the world that is slowly taking place as Dogtology spreads. Dog dentists, dog dating sites, and the proliferation of dogs-on-skateboards videos are all examples of canine-ization. Soon to come: doggie wine bars, iPaws, and canine political candidates (a definite upgrade). (2) The habit of elevating our dogs to sainthood.

Catakism. A parallel belief system to Dogtology in which the highest reverence is accorded to, ahem, cats.

CEO. The Canine Executive Officer. The true head of the household.

closet Dogtologist. A person who functionally practices Dogtology, but may not be consciously aware of it, or who may choose to keep it hidden in an attempt to have a social life (heh heh, silly human).

dogalyst. A variation (improvement) on the word "catalyst." Any event or circumstance that triggers a Canine Realization.

dog ownership. A mythical notion by which Man pretends, by the great grace of Dog, to *possess* dogs as if they were volleyballs, cans of soup, or Radio Flyer wagons. Ha!

dog-ma. The precepts and beliefs of Dogtology.

"Dog Saves." (1) A bumper sticker slogan popularized by Dogtologists. (2) The essence of Dog's relationship with Man.

dogs on skateboards. A generic term for any YouTube video of a dog pointlessly doing a human activity. The average dogs-on-skateboards video garners approximately six hundred thousand *times* more views than the average presidential speech, health and science update, or TED Talk.

Dogtological. Pertaining to, or falling under the auspices of, Dogtology.

Dogtological guilt. The belief that, through the use of sad eyes, dogs "make" humans feel guilty about forgetting to take them for walks, leaving them alone in the house for hours, and feeding them kibble that looks (and tastes) like hardened deer excrement.

Dogtologist. A practitioner of Dogtology.

Dogtology. (1) The belief in Dog. (2) The system of rituals, practices, and behaviors engaged in by Dogtologists.

douche protocol. A human social rule that states, "Humans shall treat one another with rudeness, suspicion, contempt, and total douchiness until given concrete reason to behave otherwise" (see also **Canine Law** and **Nautical Law** for exceptions to the douche protocol).

DUD. A human who Doesn't Understand Dogtology. DUDs don't necessarily dislike dogs; they just don't get what all the fuss is about (they're clueless, in other words).

eHydrants.com. An online social network for dogs, where dogs can log in; make their virtual mark; search by "casual encounters," "missed connections," or "strictly platonic"; or find their soul mate(s).

enter*train*ment. The practice of training a dog to do inane and humiliating things, such as dancing on two legs, riding a bicycle, and pretending to enjoy itself at dog shows. Strictly for human entertainment.

Fido. Originally a generic Latin term meaning "faithful," which was once inscribed over doghouses and dog guard stations. After Abe Lincoln named his dog Fido, the name came into popular usage for individual dogs (and for bargain-priced dog-food products made from insect larva and ground reptile knuckles).

Four-Wheel Bribe. A ritual by which the human, after failing to recover a runaway dog by setting out a trail of treats, screaming the dog's name until rupturing the larynx, and chasing the dog for hours on foot, must resort to tracking the dog by car, with the promise of giving the dog a ride. When the dog is ultimately duped into the car with a piece of cheese, the human must then fulfill his promise by providing the dog a minimum ten-minute car ride with its head out the window (even at 2:30 a.m.). Otherwise the Four-Wheel Bribe will fail to work in the future.

fur fix. The daily dose of Dog required by all Dogtologists. The fur fix relieves anxiety, stress, and loneliness.

human style. The face-to-face position assumed by many humans during mating sessions. Holds no attraction for dogs, who greatly prefer their own style, appropriately named.

"In Dog We Trust." The eternal motto of Dogtology.

Nautical Law. A law that states, "It is perfectly permissible (mandatory, in fact) to act friendly and outgoing toward another human being, provided at least one of the parties is aboard an aquatic vessel." Like Canine Law, Nautical Law instantly cancels out the douche protocol.

paw-aphernalia. The physical trappings of dog "ownership" that often threaten to take over the life and home of a Dogtologist (dog collars for every holiday, dog knickknacks and gadgets, dog superhero costumes, dog tanning beds, etc.).

pawspective. The art of trying to look at everyday canine/human situations from Dog's point of view.

Potty (Pawty) Party. The mysterious compulsion of dogs to join their humans in the lavatory. Clearly the dog has a strong motivation for doing this, but that motivation has remained hidden from humans since time immemorial.

power of the pups. (1) The inherent ability of Dog to change Man for the better. (Some would argue that it would be tough to change Man for the worse.) (2) The ability of dogs, by their mere presence, to put Man in a helpless emotional state in which he can only say, "Awwwww."

"Praise Dog." An expression of gratitude spontaneously uttered by Dogtologists (for example, when discovering that the doo-doo on the rug is a "hardie" and not a "softie").

quadruple octave escalation (QOE). The inexplicably high-pitched, baby-talking, slightly obsequious, walking-on-eggshells-for-no-good-reason tone of voice Dogtologists use when talking to dogs.

Rump-Sniff Daisy Chain. The potentially endless conga line that forms when one dog, followed by another, sniffs the rear of the dog in front of it. The Rump-Sniff Daisy Chain may have given rise to peaceful pack behavior in dogs, which in turn gave rise to Dog's bonding with Man, which in turn gave rise to Western civilization, which in turn gave rise to "Corporations are people, too, my friend."

Seven DUDly Sins. The list of eternal transgressions DUDs commit against dogs.

storypeeing. The secret art, mastered by dogs, unknowable by humans, of communicating complex messages through urine distribution, usually on a hydrant (see also **Whizzbook**).

"Swear to Dog." (1) The nonstop barrage of praise, vocal noises, and small talk that a Dogtologist heaps on a dog, equivalent to prayer. (2) An expression used by Dogtologists that carries the same weight as the non-Dogtologist's expression, "I swear on the grave of my sainted mother, may God strike me dead with a three-thousand-pound canned ham."

talk to Dog. The act of talking to a dog in a thoughtful, self-confessional way. A form of prayer for Dogtologists.

Ten Commands. Ten sacred guidelines handed down from Dog to Man in time immemorial to help guide Man on how to treat dogs.

twelve stages of acceptance. The steps Dogtologists go through in coming to realize that they are powerless over their dog obsession.

voice of Dog. The usually futile attempts Dog makes to communicate with Man in Dog's own natural ways, such as barking, whining, growling, and tail wagging.

Whizzbook. The *real* doggie social network (as opposed to eHydrants.com) on which dogs "post" daily comments via storypeeing. The Whizzbook network is made up primarily of fire hydrants but also includes tree stumps, rocks, car tires, kids' bicycles, and slow pedestrians.

SUNDAY SCHOOL

for Dogtologists

What are the two or three pieces of paw-aphernalia that are indispensable in any Dogtologist's home or office?
Photos are essential, of course. But if you're a serious devotee, don't limit your photo collection to only dogs you know. Put framed pictures on your walls of dogs you've only met in airports and highway restrooms. And when it comes to *that special* dog in your life, you'll need much more than just photos. You need mementos like the first batch of mail she shredded, the cunning beige pawprint she placed on your prom tuxedo and, of course, the bronzed rendition of her first grown-up poop.

Sharing images and YouTube videos of dogs is a daily ritual for Dogtologists. In fact, it's even one of the Ten Commands. But there are so many to choose from! Which links should a newly practicing Dogtologist be forwarding to others?
Dogs causing mischief when humans aren't watching is a great place to start. One recent example of this was the dog that used the kitchen table as a stepping-stone to the counter, where he spilled the bag of treats. Classic stuff. Some prefer the sweet shot of the pup sleeping next to the kitten; some like "trick" stuff like the dog barking the president's name, or the dog doing household chores; and some go

for straight action, like dogs riding skateboards or jumping on pogo sticks. And, of course, you can't go wrong with the dog in the fedora sitting at the counter drinking a cup of coffee with human hands. Just to be on the safe side, forward all of the above to everyone you've ever met.

What should a Dogtologist do when he places a festive costume piece on his dog, thinking it will delight the pup, but the dog just sits in a corner staring at him like he kicked her puppies?

One typical thing that humans do is buy sports-themed costume pieces for their dog, The human then goes around telling everyone it's the *dog* who loves the team, when in fact the dog probably hates the human's team with the white hot passion of a thousand suns and thinks they're a bunch of overpaid whiners, but doesn't know how to break the news to the human politely. After all, the human is the dog's connection to treats. If you've done this to a dog, you must make amends. Try wearing something that's meaningful to your dog, like earmuffs made of bacon, or pajamas with dead goldfish stapled to them. That should bring her around.

Whizzbook is the "social network" for dogs, where peeing on things equals "posting" and sniffing equals reading (Book of Hydrants, IV). What's "trending" on Whizzbook lately?

There's talk about some female teacup Chihuahua hooking up with a male St. Bernard that's causing all kinds of wild speculation. On the fashion front we're seeing a goth trend in poodle cuts that is causing cats to spontaneously question the meaning of existence. And there have been attempts to organize a group squat on the White House lawn to protest the cheap materials being used in doggy bumblebee costumes, but nothing has been confirmed yet.

As is well known, the rift between Dogtologists and followers of Catakism has caused a great historical schism in the world. These ancient rivals made great strides toward peace in the twentieth

century, but tensions remain. **What does the next century look like for Dogtology/Cataksim relations?**

What was once a ferociously boiling pot has now been turned down to a slow simmer, and that's good news for peace on Earth. The cause of this newfound détente has been the ability of some humans to embrace both beliefs. This may seem like blasphemy to some, but modern man has found a way to bridge the gap between Cataksim and Dogtology by elevating *both* species to positions of outright worship while simultaneously reducing the treatment of fellow humans to that of beetle manure (see "douche protocol" in *Fur*minology).

When Dogtologists commit one or more of the Seven DUDly Sins, what's the best way for them to get back on track? How does a Dogtologist practice penance?

Nobody is perfect, and we all slip over to the dark side during weak moments. Sometimes we do the fake ball throw and then pretend we were just stretching our shoulder muscle. Or we interrupt a dog's butt scootch with a cry of "Eww! Gross!" and then act like we were yelling at a topical ointment commercial on TV. But Dog knows. And Dog forgives. Of course, occasionally Dog must remind us of our transgressions by filing an opinion statement on our cashmere rug or suede shoes. And then all we can do is repent for our sins by leaving the shepherd's pie near the edge of the counter to cool while we go to the mall.

There's been a recent crop of books by luminaries skeptical of or downright hostile toward Dogtology. Richard Pawkins's *The Dog Delusion* and Christopher Hoochins's *Dog Is Not Great* come to mind. Should Dogtologists be concerned about this rising tide of secularism—or does it only strengthen their faith?

These books are written by the extremists. Every belief has its radical sect. Just as Dogtology has its fanatical "dog show" contingent, DUDs have their own anti-Dog zealots. These DUDs are to be pitied rather than reviled, for between the lines of their rabid dog denouncements one can hear the sad strains of a lost soul who was simply deprived of doggy love in childhood.

The hosts of *The 700 Kennel* encourage viewers to tithe their income for charity. To which charitable organizations should Dogtologists donate?

Dogtology, as a belief system, allows believers to support the love of Dog in any way they choose. Tithing is an interesting concept, but dogs show remarkably little interest in money (evidence for this: after eating your entire wallet they unfailingly leave your paycheck scattered in Tic Tac-sized fragments across your lawn). If you happen to work for an employer who pays in tennis balls, Milk Bones, and small chunks of raw hamburger, then, by all means, consider tithing. That said, if cash is all you have to work with, a few organizations come to mind: Doctors Without Border Collies, The Salivation Army, Greenpee, Hamnesty International, Make a Dish Foundation . . .

At the end of *Dogtology*, Dog tells humans, "There's more to me than you've even begun to suspect." What does this cryptic message mean?

Some questions are too deep to be given simple answers. It's not the role of any Dogtologist to interpret the faith for another. It's up to individual devotees to decide what Dog means to them in their own lives. This takes a heart wide open with seeking spirit, and a pocket wide open with Liv-a-Snaps.

Any recommendations for further reading for Dogtologists interested in learning even more about their faith?

Every book on the subject of dogs is about Dogtology, regardless of its angle. The fact that we write so many books about Dog and dogs is a clear demonstration of how much we love them and obsess over them. This particular book, *Dogtology*, represents the first attempt to formally set down the dog-trine and dog-ma of the faith, but the book has really been in the works since Man first met Dog. As a dog-driven society, we continue to evolve our beliefs and to find new ways of practicing and celebrating Dogtology. Thus we will all continue to write the next volume of Dogtology together.

ABOUT THE AUTHOR'S DOG

I wasn't in the market for a dog, but he was mine in an instant. He came to me as a stray pup and we bonded like Gorilla Glue. Cutest face ever—with a personality to match. Olympic athlete, President of the Canine Mensa Society, the James Dean of dogs. A performer—like me—but superior, of course.

The Golden Boy. Rocket Dog. The Rebel With the Paws. The Urinator. He was a multi-faceted canine—with many monikers to match.

Every time I caught his eye, he grinned. We were always playing at outsmarting and outmaneuvering each other. It was Rocket Dog: 748, me: 11. But the moment I sat on the couch, he would jump on my lap and lick my face; then we were even.

The Golden Boy (he was as good as his color), became my confidant, my sidekick, my BFF. I found I could be truer with him than with anyone else; so I wanted to hang with him day and night. He became my refuge, my sanity, my partner in crime.

One night, while out on a first date that was going suspiciously well, my dinner partner surprised me by grabbing the third rail of dating and asking, point-blank, what my religion was. Crap. There it was. Out of the bag and demanding an unequivocal response. Just to be funny and preserve some hope for a happy ending, I blurted out, "Dogtology."

It was only later I realized that I'd spoken more truth than I intended. My belief in Dog truly was the only real constant in my life. That's when I had my Canine Realization: My love for the

Golden Fur Angel blossomed into an insane love and reverence for dogs—for all Dogkind.

I wasn't just a lover of dogs, I realized, I was a bleepin' devotee. Suddenly, where I had previously been blind to my faith, I could see it everywhere: paws on shirts, bone-shaped pillows, hydrant cookies. This planet is a bone-a-fide temple to Dog! Oh my Dog, how had I missed this all along?

Dogtology. Howl-elujah!

ACKNOWLEDGMENTS

This dogtrine would not be made possible without the endless love and support from D.E. and the friendship from A.W.

To Roamy . . . My Inspiration. Forever wrapped around your paw.